A WORD AT THE START.

This monograph on *The Irish Scots and The " Scotch-Irish"* was originally prepared by me for *The Granite Monthly*, of Concord, N. H. It was published in that magazine in three successive instalments which appeared, respectively, in the issues of January, February and March, 1888. With the exception of a few minor changes, the monograph is now reproduced as originally written.

The paper here presented on *How the Irish Came as Builders of The Nation* is based on articles contributed by me to the Boston *Pilot* in 1890, and at other periods, and on an article contributed by me to the Boston Sunday *Globe* of March 17, 1895.

The *Supplementary Facts and Comment*, forming the conclusion of this publication, will be found of special interest and value in connection with the preceding sections of the work.

JOHN C. LINEHAN.

Concord, N. H., July 1, 1902.

HON. JOHN C. LINEHAN.

The Irish Scots and the "Scotch-Irish"

An Historical and Ethnological Monograph

With Some Reference to
Scotia Major and Scotia Minor

To Which is Added a Chapter on
"How the Irish Came as Builders of the Nation"

By
Hon. John C. Linehan

State Insurance Commissioner of New Hampshire
Member, the New Hampshire Historical Society
Treasurer-General, American-Irish Historical Society
Late Department Commander, New Hampshire, Grand Army of the Republic
Many Years a Director of the Gettysburg Battlefield Association

HERITAGE BOOKS
2007

THE IRISH SCOTS AND THE "SCOTCH-IRISH."

A STUDY of peculiar interest to all of New Hampshire birth and origin is the early history of those people, who, differing from the settlers around them, were first called Irish by their English neighbors, "Scotch-Irish" by some of their descendants, and later on "Scotch" by writers like Mr. Morrison of Windham, N. H.

According to the latter, "The ignorance of other classes in relation to them and their history was unbounded." "They were called Irish, when not a drop of Irish blood flowed in their veins." "They were of Scotch blood, pure and simple; the blood of Erin did *not* flow commingled in the veins of the hardy exiles, who, one hundred and sixty and more years ago, struck for a settlement and a home in this wintry land." "Then let every descendant of the first settlers distinctly remember that his ancestors were Scotch, that he is of Scotch descent, and that the terms 'Scotch-Irish' and 'Scotch-English,' so far as they imply a different than Scotch origin and descent, are a perversion of truth and false to history."

Many have heard of what the old lady said, "There's where St. Paul and I differ," and, like that argumentative, kindly old soul, there is where Mr. Morrison and history differ. The American of English origin, who is fortunate in tracing his lineage to the Mayflower and Plymouth Rock, is not content to stop there. He goes back to Britain, and even then is not satisfied until he goes to the

cradle of his race in Germany, the home of the Saxon; so
would the true Scot go back to the Highlands, and from
thence across to the home of *his* race, Ireland, the true
Scotia of history, the source of his language, his customs,
manners, laws, name and religion.   That this is not more
generally known is not the fault of history but of prejudice, and after all not surprising, for where among modern
nations can be found a people more vilified and more persecuted, and whose early history has been more misrepre-
sented or studiously avoided than that of the ancient Irish
and their descendants?   A criticism of the London *Times*,
quite recently, on a work on Ireland by a young English
student, was very severe because the writer went back of
the Norman invasion, which the *Times* said was of no
possible interest to Englishmen.   It is not uncommon to
find occasionally a child ashamed to own its parent, but
that does not by any means sever the relationship; and
writers like those mentioned, so proud of their alleged
Scotch origin, cannot, even if they would, rob Erin of her
ancient name and appropriate it to themselves without
giving credit were it is due.   As well might the people of
New England attempt to take to themselves the name,
fame and glory of the older England and deny it to the
latter.

Cochrane*, in his " History of Antrim, N. H.," speaks in
glowing terms of his Highland ancestors — of their uncon-
querable, haughty natures, of their bravery to the foe, and
their kindness to the poor, but repudiates the idea of their

* It is probable that the name Cochrane derives from O'Corcoran. The O'Corcorans
were of the Clan Cian of Ormond (now the County Tipperary) in the Irish Province of
Munster. The MacCorcorans are also mentioned in Ormond and Desies (Tipperary and
Waterford) as chiefs of the Clan Rooney. An Irish form of O'Corcoran was O'Corcrain.
The name has been anglicized Corcoran, Coghrane, Cockran, etc. The late Gen. John
Cochrane, of New York, was a member of the American-Irish Historical Society, and a
descendant of a patriot officer of the American Revolution. Hon. W. Bourke Cockran, the
distinguished orator, is another representative of the clan.

Irish origin; but a standard Scotch work, the writers in which being on the ground ought to know whereof they speak, tells the story as follows (vol. ii, p. 333, Chamber's, Encyclopædia): "The 'Scots' were the Celtic tribes in Scotland, dwelling in the western and more mountainous districts north of the Forth and the Clyde, who, when it became necessary to distinguish them from the Teutonic inhabitants of the low country, received the names of the 'Wild Scots,' 'The Irishry of Scotland,' and more recently the 'Scotch Highlanders.' " St. Bridget," it also mentions, "was held in great reverence in Scotland, and was regarded by the Douglasses as their tutelary saint." In their respect for St. Patrick *, also, the Scots of the Highlands were not a whit behind their kindred in Ireland, as the frequent mention of the name proves.

In these latter days a new school of writers has sprung up, whose pride of ancestry outstrips their knowledge, and whose prejudices blind their love of truth. With the difference in religion between certain sections of the Irish people as a basis, they are bent on creating a new race, christening it 'Scotch-Irish,' laboring hard to prove that it is a 'brand' superior to either of the two old types, and while clinging to the Scotch root, claim that their ancestors were different from the Irish in blood, morals, language and religion. This is a question not difficult to settle for those who are disposed to treat it honestly, but, as a rule, the writers who are the most prolific, as well as the speakers who are the most eloquent, know the least about the subject, and care less, if they can only succeed in having their theories accepted. The Irish origin of the Scots is studiously avoided by nearly all the "Scotch-Irish" writers,

---

* Patrick was for a long period a favorite Christian name among the Scottish Highlanders and was proudly borne by many of their greatest men.

or if mentioned at all, is spoken of in a manner which leaves the reader to infer that the Scots had made a mistake in selecting their ancestors, and it was the duty of their descendants, so far as it lay in their power, to rectify the error.

There was so much prejudice shown towards the Londonderry, N. H., settlers by the English of the adjoining towns, that Rev. Mr. McGregor, their pastor, according to Belknap or Barstow, wrote Governor Shute complaining because they were called Irish Catholics when they had been loyal to the British Empire and fought against the papists; but it is recorded also that he wrote to the French governor of Canada that his people were from Ireland, and craved his good graces with the Indians; and in this he was more successful than in the former, for while the hostility of the English settlers lasted for years, the Londonderry people were not molested by the Indians, who made havoc with their neighbors all around them.

St. Donatus, or Donough, Bishop of Fiesole, in the seventh century, one of the band of missionaries, whose names are found all over the continent of Europe, describes his country as follows :

> " Far westward lies an isle of ancient fame,
> By nature blessed, and Scotia is her name
> Enrolled in books, — exhaustless in her store
> Of veiny silver and of golden ore.
> Her fruitful soil forever teems with wealth,
> With gems her waters, and her air with health ;
> Her verdant fields with milk and honey flow,
> Her woolly fleeces vie with virgin snow ;
> Her waving furrows float with bearded corn,
> And arms and arts her envied sons adorn ;
> No savage bear with lawless fury roves,
> Nor ravenous lion through the peaceful groves ;
> No poison there infects, no scaly snake
> Creeps through the grass, nor frog annoys the lake —
> An island worthy of her pious race,
> In war triumphant, and unmatched in peace."

"Conradus, a Monte Puellarum, who wrote about 1340, states that men illustrious for sanctity flourished in Ireland, which was called Scotia Major; and Grester, Canisius, Cæsarius, Marianus Scotus, Orosius, Isodorus, and Venerable Bede, with a train of other learned writers, who flourished from the sixth until the fourteenth century, designate Ireland by the appellation of Scotia; and the Breviary of Aberdeen in Scotland shows, beyond all controversy, that there was a Scotia Minor as well as a Scotia Major. In this ancient Breviary it is mentioned that 'St. Winnius, born in a province of Scotia from the illustrious Neillian monarchs, was by a prosperous and propitious gale wafted to Scotia Minor.'"

Two Scoto-Irish saints, according to Chambers, vol. iv., p. 324, "have left their mark on the topography of Ireland and Scotland—St. Fillian the Leper and St. Fillian the Abbot." The former had a church on Loch Erne in Perthshire, Scotland, and another in Ballyheyland, Ireland. The latter had a church in Westmeath, Ireland, and in the upper part of Glendochart, Perthshire, Scotland, which takes from him the name of Strathfillian. St. Fillian's well takes its name from the former. A relic of St. Fillian the Abbot has been preserved to our time, the silver head of his Crosier or pastoral staff now in possession of a member of the family, Alexander Davar, a farmer in Canada, whose ancestors have been the hereditary and legal custodians of the relic since the thirteenth century. A full description of it, "the Quigrich or Crosier of St. Fillian," will be found in the proceedings of the Society of Antiquaries of Scotland, (Edin., 1861).

Of the language—Gaelic—Mr. Richard Garnett, one of the most learned of English philologists, states,—

"That Irish is the parent tongue; that Scottish Gaelic is Irish stripped of a few inflections; and that the language of the Highlands does not differ in any essential point from that of the opposite coast of Leinster or Ulster, bearing in fact a closer resemblance than low German does to high German, or Danish to Swedish."

Mr. W. F. Skene, one of the best informed of Scottish writers on the Gaelic language, although laboring hard to find a native origin for it, has to admit that the north of Ireland, the Scottish Highlands, and west islands were, at an early age, peopled by the same race; and further admits, that from the middle of the twelfth century to about the middle of the sixteenth century, Ireland exercised a powerful literary influence on the Scottish Highlands; that the Irish sennachies and bards were heads of a school which included the west Highlands; that the Highland sennachies were either of Irish descent, or, if they were of native origin, resorted to the schools in Ireland for instruction in the language; that in this way the language and literature of the Scottish Highlands must have become more and more assimilated to the language and literature of Ireland; and that it may well be doubted whether, towards the middle of the sixteenth century, there existed in the Scottish Highlands the means of acquiring the art of writing the language except in Ireland, or the conception of a written and cultivated literature which was not identified with the language of that island."

The first printed books, from 1567 to 1690, for the use of the Scottish Highlanders, were all in the Irish orthography and Irish dialect,—a translation of the Bible in 1690 being simply a reprint of Bishop Bedel's Irish version of the same. Here, then, is proof sufficient that from the middle of the sixteenth century, back to the dawn of modern history, Ireland and Scotland, the mother and daughter, were closely connected—one in blood, language, and religion. The Reformation brought about a change of faith, but that would not transform the blood.

The Scots from Argylshire, who went to Ireland under James the First in 1612–'20, were the ancestors of the so-called "Scotch-Irish" of New Hampshire; and it will be hard for writers like Mr. Cochrane or Mr. Morrison to prove that "the blood of Erin did *not* flow commingled in their veins," for the writings of Skene and other Scotchmen admit the close connection almost down to the departure of the Argyle emigrants for Ulster ; and the names borne by the greater part of the settlers were those peculiar to the Highlands and to Ireland.

Buckle's " History of Civilization," speaking of Scotland, says:—" It is at this point— the withdrawal of the Romans — that we begin to discern the physical and geographical peculiarities of Scotland. The Romans gradually losing ground, the proximity of Ireland caused repeated attacks from that fertile island, whose rich soil and great natural advantages gave rise to an exuberant, and therefore restless, population. An overflow which in civilized times is an emigration, is in barbarous times an invasion. Hence the Irish, or Scotti as they were termed, established themselves by force of arms in the west of Scotland, and came into collision with the Picts, who occupied the eastern part. A deadly struggle ensued, which lasted four centuries after the withdrawal of the Romans, and plunged the country into the greatest confusion. At length, in the middle of the ninth century,

Kenneth McAlpin, king of the Scotti, gained the upper hand, and reduced the Picts to complete subjection. The country was then united under one rule, and the conquerors, slowly absorbing the conquered, gave their name to the whole, which in the tenth century received the appellation of Scotland."

Pinkerton, in his "Ancient Lives of Scottish Saints," speaking of the Picts, says that "Pictavia is spoken of by the chronicles long after the accession of Kenneth McAlpin, and *long before Scotia became idenified with northern Britain, or ceased to be the ordinary name of Ireland.*" Again he writes, — "The Picts, supposed by some to be the Caledonians of the Roman writers, when first known under that name, occupied the whole territory north of the Firth of Forth except the western portion, which had been colonized or subdued by the Scots, another Celtic nation, whose chief seat was in Ireland, — *the proper and ancient Scotland.*" "The Southern Picts were converted to Christianity by St. Ninnian, and the Northern Picts by St. Columba," two of the most celebrated of the Irish missionaries of the sixth century.

Fergus, son of Erc, (Mac Earca) — from whence the Fergusons derive their name — the first king of the British Scots, was supposed to be a close connection of St. Columbkille. For his coronation the stone of destiny (in Ireland known as the "Lia Fail," in Scotland "The Stone of Scone") was brought to the Highlands from Ireland, but not returned according to promise, and for years was kept in the church of Scone, where the Scottish sovereigns were crowned, down to the time of Edward I., king of England, who captured and conveyed it to England, where it now forms part of the coronation chair of the sovereigns of the United Kingdom in Westminster Abbey. From Edward to Victoria every ruler of Britian has been crowned on the stone. Even Cromwell, the Puritan, too democratic to go into the abbey, had the chair brought out into the hall, and on it took the oath of office as "Lord Protector" of England.

Of the absurdity of the statement that the blood of any nation is pure, "free from commingling," a writer in Chambers, vol. xi, p. 382, says, — "It is unreasonable to suppose that the Anglo-Saxon invaders exterminated the native Celtic population (of Britain), or even drove more than a tithe of them into the Highlands. The mass undoubtedly remained as subject serfs, learned the language and customs of their masters, and gradually amalgamated with them, so that perhaps, in point of blood, the English are as much Celtic as Teutonic."

The invasion of England later by the Norman French proves the theory of this writer. The Saxons were enslaved by their masters, and in time amalgamated with them, so that to-day the language as well as the blood shows the mixture. In fact, there are more French than Saxon words in the former ; and writers of Alfred's period would esteem themselves, in the England of to-day, so far as the mother tongue is concerned, strangers in a strange land.

Green, in his work, "The Making of England," a most admirable book, confines himself to the period between the landing of Henghist and Horsa, in 449, to the union of all England under Alfred, about 850. From the Angles, Saxons, Danes, and Jutes, mixed with a remnant of the ancient Britons, and from the Norman French, who invaded England in 1040 under William the Conqueror, are descended the English people. The language, on account of the mixture of races, is to-day, according to Max Muller, the most composite of any spoken on the globe, the number of words in Webster's and standard English dictionaries derived from the Latin or French being in the proportion of two to one from the Saxon.

Now the man who *is* to write the "Making of Scotland," following the plan of Green, will find, according to the testimony of that writer, who derived his knowledge from Gildas, the last British historian, and from various other authorities whom he quotes, that the coast of Britain, under the Roman power, was continually raided by the Scots of Ireland; that they had established colonies on various points, north and south ; that between the second and third centuries the kingdom of Dalriada was founded by them in what was then called Caledonia: that in company with the Picts, the aborigines of Scotland, they used to pour down on the Romans from the Highlands; that to keep them out the Emperor Severus built the great Roman wall; that on the decline of the Roman power, and after being driven out of Dalriada, the Scots again passed over from Ireland, under Fergus, son of Erc, who was crowned first king of the British Scots in 503.

From this time up to about the date of the accession of Alfred, the condition of Caledonia was similar to that of England, continual warfare between the Scots and Picts ending in the complete subjection of the latter in the eighth century, and the crowning of Kenneth McAlpin as the first king of Scotland. The Picts disappear from the pages of history ; no trace of language or custom remains. From Ireland the Scots took their traditions, manners, religion, laws, customs, language, and name.

Chamber's Encyclopedia, vol. ii, p. 712, says of the Caledonians,— "Whether of the Cymric or Erse branch of the Celts is unknown, they disappear in the third century. The same doubt exists in regard to the Picts, but the Scots were emigrants from Ireland, both Scots and Gael being common names of the old Irish." Again, speaking of Scotland, vol. 7, p. 555: " The original Scotia or Scotland was Ireland, and the Scoti or Scots, the people of Ireland, a Celtic race." For many years, owing to the confusion incidental to the two kindred peoples, their nations were known to continental writers as Scotia Major and Scotia Minor. The exact period when the name ceased to be applied to Ireland is unknown, but is supposed to be about the twelfth century. From the Irish people, according to Chambers, "the Anglo-Saxons received their knowledge of religion mainly, and of letters entirely."

Green gives credit to the same source, and wrote that " It was the fashion in Europe in the ninth century to go to Ireland for piety and learning." Scottish scholars and ecclesiastics from Ireland not only flooded pagan England, but spread all over Europe. A Saxon raid on the coast of Ireland in the eighth century, according to Green, was looked upon as a sacrilege by the English people, an outrage on the land from which came their teachers and benefactors. Columb-kill at Iona, Columban in France and Lombardy, Gall in Switzerland, and hundreds of their associate Scots, carried the gospel of Christ and a knowledge of the classics to the then pagan countries of northern Europe and the older nations of the south, whose faith had been corrupted and whose knowledge of learning impaired by the repeated inroads of the barbarians.

The language of the England of to-day was not that of
the Angles, who were entirely ignorant of letters. The
blood of the modern Anglo-Saxon is not as clear as that
of his ancestors of the fifth century. The names of the
people are not the same as those in use a thousand years
ago, but, according to all English writers, they are the
same people, and on that question no issue is desired.
But apply the same rule to the Scotch, the language of the
Highlands is the same Gaelic, without corruption or mixture, that their ancestors used when they left Ireland. It
is the same tongue used in Ireland to-day where Irish is
spoken. Their family names are those largely used in
Ireland before Anglo-Saxons had acquired a knowledge of
the alphabet, or knew how to make the sign of the cross,
both of which were taught them by the Scottish missionaries. The Mac is known only in Ireland and Scotland, or
in countries peopled by those nations. The connection
between the people of both countries was close, down to
the Reformation*. On Ireland the British Scots had to
depend for education. They had no schools of their own;
the seats of learning were all in the old land, at Armagh,
Bangor, Derry, Cashel, and other places of note in those
days; and even as late as the sixteenth century the Highland harpers went to Ireland to get a musical education.

When the Scots emigrated from Ireland, the memory of
St. Patrick was fresh in their minds; the precepts he
taught were what they practised. His name, with that of

---

* So close was this connection, that Edward Bruce, brother of Robert, was at one period
invited to come to Ireland and become king of the latter country. The invitation was
accepted. Edward landed near Carrickfergus A. D. 1315, with a force of 6000 Scots. He
was immediately joined by O'Neill and other great Irish lords of the north, and soon by
O'Connor, king of Connaught, O'Brien of Thomond, and other Irish leaders of the east,
west and south. Bruce was crowned king of Ireland at Dundalk with impressive cere-
monies. The Irish and Scotch allies then vigorously proceeded against the English in
Ireland, speedily drove them out of Ulster, and then marched southward, defeating the
English in several pitched battles.

Bridget, was loved and honored in Scotland, and revered in Ireland. The Saxons even, loved the name of Bridget, which was borne by one of Cromwell's daughters, and it will also be found on the the tombstones of the Walker family in Concord, N. H., in the old cemetery.

In no part of the world was the Celtic blood more vigorous than in the Highlands, where, in Argylshire, as late as 1851, with a population of about 90,000, mostly all used the Gaelic tongue. The Scotch are then more truly Celtic than the English are Saxon ; and it is unfair, in the light of history, to draw a line between them and their kindred of Ireland.

It is the fashion now among some people, to do this, and among the number who wish to cut off the connection, if such a thing were possible, are the offspring of many whose ancestors never saw the hills of Scotland, but who would fain enroll themselves in the ranks of the "Scotch-Irish."

From Ireland to Ardh-Gaehdal (Argyle) the Scots went in 503. To Ireland from Argyle returned the Scots in 1612–'20 ; and to America their descendants sailed away in 1719. Call them "Scotch-Irish," or "Scotch," as you will, this is their record. If it is wrong, then the scholarly writers in Chambers are mistaken, and Green's works full of errors. That the people of the Lowlands are mixed will make no difference. Apply the same rule to both countries, and Scotland, as we have said, is more Celtic than England is Saxon. Another fact in connection with this point is of interest. Cochrane, in his history of Antrim, N. H., alluding to the "Massacre" of 1641, states that but comparatively few of the Scotch were killed by the Irish, whose hatred was more directly against the

English, and also wrote that while the English settlements were repeatedly attacked by the French and Indians in New Hampshire, the "Scotch-Irish" were not molested, and that there was a supposition that they had been instructed to that effect by the Jesuit priests in Canada; rather suggestive.

The "Massacre" of 1641 has been for years a favorite weapon in the hands of those who dislike the Irish Catholics; but it has been treated so often by Irish Protestants who love the truth and the good name of their countrymen, that a word from one whose ancestors have been so foully slandered for two hundred years is not needed. The "History of Ireland," by Prof. Taylor, of Trinity college, Dublin, published by Harper Brothers; "Vindiciæ Hibernicæ," by Mathew Carey, father of the great writer on political economy, Henry C. Carey; and the "Cromwellian Settlement," by John P. Prendergast, — all deal exhaustively with the subject.

For over eighty years, under the reigns of the Jameses, Cromwell, the two Charleses, and William the Third, the "Scotch-Irish" so-called, had been the willing instruments in the hands of English rulers and English parliaments to uphold the English power and the English church. Presbyterians themselves, they fought willingly against their Catholic kindred for their share of the land of Ireland. And no matter what was the religion professed by their masters, or the form of government, — monarchy or republic, king or protector, Episcopal or Puritan, — they did their full part; but the day of reckoning came, and bitterly did they reap the fruit of their labors and sacrifices. The surrender of Limerick ended the terrible struggle so far as the Irish Catholics were concerned. William was firmly seated on the throne, the Irish for the first time completely subjugated. their lands in the possession of the enemy, the troopers of Cromwell and of William, and their persons at the mercy of all who hated them.

The French Protestants, who fought for William with his Dutch auxiliaries, had settled in Ireland; many of them were skilled artisans. Manufactures sprang up; the war was over, and the arts of peace followed; the herds of cattle, sheep, and horses increased. The lot of the poor Irish people was growing better; their services—their labor—were required; and it seemed after all as if the country was going to see peace and prosperity restored, although confined mainly to the strangers. But, lo and behold! the people of England awoke one morning and found a new competitor crowding them in their own markets. They had been accustomed to supply the Irish people; but the tables were turned, and England was flooded with Irish cattle, Irish wool, and Irish woolens. That would never do. Parliament was appealed to; the prayers of the English merchants were granted; the exportation of cattle and manufactured goods from Ireland was forbidden; and the great British nation was once more saved. This was a hard blow to the loyal Protestants, in whose hands and by whose exertions Ireland in so short a time had proved to be so formidable a rival. Ireland— Protestant Ireland—sank under it.

Then, again, the government finding the Presbyterians independent and stiff-necked, and having for the time being effectually settled the Catholic question, exporting to the West India islands and to New England over ten thousand boys and girls, young men and women, and scattering over Europe, from Italy to Poland, additional thousands of exiles,—soldiers, priests, and laymen,—turned its paternal eyes on the Presbyterian Irish of the North, and it took but a few years for them to learn,—after restrictions placed on their religion, petty persecution of their pastors, the increase of their rents on leases expiring, and the entire destruction of their manufacturing industries,— that it made but little difference* with the English government what people it was that inhabited Hibernia,—the old Irish, the "Norman-Irish," the "Anglo-Saxon-Irish," or the "Scotch-Irish." Their mission in life according to the government was to work for the profit of the English people, to fight, and, if necessary, to die for the English government, and to worship God in conformity with the English church.

What was the result? Why, those people whose ancestors left Scotland one hundred or more years before turned their backs on Ireland, and in thousands emigrated to America, accompanied by fully as many of the old race, whose homes were found all over the original thirteen colonies, and whose descendants are found today throughout the country—the McNeils, McLeans, Lanahans, Carrols, Lynches, McMurphys, McGregors, Barrys, Sullivans, McCormicks, McDuffys, O'Briens, Manahans, O'Neils, O'Donnells, Brannans, Pollocks, Buchanans, Morrisons, McClintocks, McGuires, McCarthys, Jacksons, Coffees, Groghans, McGradys, Clarkes, Harneys, McDonoughs, Porters, McMillans, Montgomerys, Shutes, O'Haras, McAffees, McGinnises, McGowans, Butlers, Fitzgeralds, Mooneys, Kellys, Kennys, Moores, Gilmores, McAdoos, Kearneys, Haleys,

* During the Irish Revolution of 1798, hosts of Irish Presbyterians nobly identified themselves with the patriot cause. Many Presbyterian ministers were seized by the British enemy and executed as "rebels" to English law.

McClarys, Pendergasts, Sheas, Roaches, McCombs, Mc-
Calls, McGills, McRaes, Kanes, Flynns, O'Connors, Mc-
Clellans, McClanahans, McGees, O'Keefes, O'Rourkes,
O'Reillys, McConihes, McDougals, McDowells, etc., etc.
Many immortalized themselves by deeds of daring in the
service of the colonies or the republic, on land and on sea.

Lord Fitzwilliam estimated the number of operatives
who left Ireland at one hundred thousand. Dobbs' " History of Irish Trade," Dublin, 1727, said that three thousand males left Ulster yearly for the colonies. Philadelphia
alone, for the year 1729, shows a record of 5,655 Irish
emigrants, against English and Welsh, 267 ; Scotch, 43 ;
Germans, 343.

They left Ireland with the most intense hatred of England. That hatred was religiously transmitted to their
children, which England found to her cost in the war of
the Revolution, the close of which found Moylan the commander of the dragoons, and Hand the adjutant-general of
the army — both natives of Ireland. Among those of
their kindred who remained at home this intensity of feeling found vent in the institution of the order of " United
Irishmen," first composed, like the Charitable Irish Society
of Boston (founded, 1737), of Protestants, afterwards assimi-
lating with those of the Catholic faith, and culminating in
the Rebellion of 1798, when for the first time in the history of Ireland the Catholic and Protestant Celts fought
on the same side, and the Catholic priest and Presbyterian
elder were hanged on the same tree. This is so well
known that no authorities need be quoted.

The so-called " Scotch-Irish" loved Ireland. Their action
in 1798 proved that they did not hate her sons ; and they
emigrated to America, not as some writers would have the

world believe, on account of dislike to the Irish Catholics, but because they could not live under the English govern-ment in Ireland.

The affinity between the kindred races is treated lightly by modern writers, especially in New Hampshire, and the saying of Bayard Taylor, in " Picturesque Europe," that "they [the Irish] were the true Scots of history," would no doubt be exceedingly distasteful to them ; but it will be very hard to find a Teutonic origin for the gallant and stubborn race which has never learned to bend the knee or bow the head to tyrants, either in Ireland or in Scotland — a race to which Europe owes a debt it can never repay. For from the teachings of the Scots, at a time when Rome and Greece were overrun by barbaric hosts, Scotland learned her duty to the true God as taught by the gospel of His divine Son, and acquired a knowledge of letters which, owing to the overthrow of Rome, was fast dying out elsewhere.

Cochrane in his History of Antrim, N. H., and Morrison in his History of Windham and the History of the Morrison Family, allude to the theory of the Irish origin of the Scotch, but do not consider it credible. A study, how-ever, of the origin of the names of persons and places in Ireland and Scotland would easily disclose the relationship. The prefixes Kin, Kil, and Dun in the names of places are as frequent in one country as in the other, and the prefixes Mac and Kil to the names of persons are common to both. Mac simply means son, — MacShane, son of John ; Mac-Donough, son of Dennis ; MacGregor, son of Gregory ; MacDermot or MacDiarmid, son of Jeremiah ; MacDonald, son of Daniel ; MacPhadrig, son of Patrick ; MacTeague, son of Timothy; MacBride, son of Bridget ; MacMurrough, son of Murrough, etc.

The prefix Kil, so often seen in Irish names of persons and places, and also peculiar to Scotland, is not as sanguinary as it appears. It is the Celtic pronunciation of cell — the *c* being hard in Gaelic, and the word being pronounced as if spelled *kel*. So comes the name Kilpatrick or cell of Patrick, Kilmichael, Kildare, etc.

The ancient name ot Edinburgh was Dun-Eidan. Dunmore, Dunluce and Dungiven in Ireland, will be matched by Dunbarton, Dundonald and Dundee in Scotland.

The prefix and affix Ross is also peculiar to both countries. Melross (Melrose) Abbey in Scotland and Muckross Abbey in Ireland show the relation : it means headland.

In Ireland a lake is called a lough — Lough Erne ; in Scotland, a loch — Loch Lomond ; — so with the names of mountains, etc., etc. A slight knowledge of the Gaelic language would be of inestimable value, especially to Mr. Morrison, who would not then be obliged to draw such heavy drafts on his imagination in seeking for the origin of the Morrison family ; for certainly, before the Teutonic Mohrs, from which he fondly hopes he has sprung, left their native wilds of Germania, or before the Blessed Virgin found followers in Ireland or in the Highlands of Scotland so devoted as to style themselves sons of Mary — Marysons — the MacMurroughs of Leinster (sons of Murrough or Murroughsons)* did many a deed of bravery.

* In addition to Maryson and Murroughson, other origins are found for the Irish name Morrison. Thomas Hamilton Murray, while editor of the Daily Sun, Lawrence., Mass., wrote, in June, 1896, a paper on "The Irish Morrisons. Eminent in Ancient, Mediæval and Modern Times. A Glance at the Origin of the Clan Name, Together with Reference to the Family's Patrimony in the Ancient Kingdom of Connaught." He states on the authority of O'Hart that Diarmaid, who is No. 111 on the MacDermot (princes of Moylurg) pedigree, had two brothers, Donoch and Teige Oge. Donoch was the ancestor of O'Muirios and MacMuirios, which have been anglicized O'Morris, O'Morrison, MacMorris, etc., and from which derive such names as MacMorrissey, Morrissey, Morrison, Morison and various others. Other Irish Morris and Morrison families trace their descent from Tiomain Muirios, whose brother Tiobrad is No. 91 on the O'Dowd pedigree. Tiomain flourished early in the sixth century. In the list of "Irish chiefs and clans" given by O'Hart, O'Morrison is mentioned among those in Mayo and Sligo. O'Hart also mentions the O'Morrisons of Donegal. He likewise states that a member of the Irish O'Morris or MacMorris (MacMorris — son of Morris, i e., Morrison), family settled in Scotland at an early period, and was the ancestor of Morrison there.

One thing is certain, and it is this, to the unprejudiced reader: it does not appear from a perusal of colonial documents that these people who settled in Londonderry and other towns in New Hampshire were so much ashamed of being called Irish as the writings of some of their descendants indicate. There were scattered among them many bearing names peculiar to the east, west and south of Ireland, like Flynn, Lanahan, O'Brien, Manahan, Sullivan, Lynch, Connor, Mooney, Burke and Fitzgerald, as well as such well known north of Ireland names as O'Neill, McMahon and O'Donnell. In addition, the settlers of Scotch origin were largely the descendants of those who settled in Ireland in 1612–'20, one hundred years or more before the emigration to America, and inter-marriages had taken place between them and their ancient relatives.

It is not then surprising that their newly settled towns were named after the dear old homes, not in Scotland, but in Ireland; that the society organized in Boston in 1737 was called the Charitable Irish Society instead of the Scotch; that the second Masonic lodge in New Hampshire was named St. Patrick's Lodge, and was instituted on St. Patrick's Day, in the year 1780, and not on St. Andrew's Day; that the first grand master of the order in the state was John Sullivan; and that some of the most eminent men in the land sprung from this noted stock. As there was also considerable emigration direct from Scotland to America, and as for a great many noted men is claimed affinity, not directly with the Scotch, but rather with the "Scotch-Irish," it must be granted that the sojourn of a hundred years or more in Ireland, and the intermarriages with the people of that country, produced a superior race, which should be called, according to the rule humorously laid down by Gov. Ames of Massachusetts, at a banquet of the Charitable Irish Society, " The improved order of Scotchmen," as he styled them—the members of the Charitable Society—" The improved order of Irishmen." But, to be serious, as history has been written about the so-called "Scotch-Irish" here in New Hampshire, an Irishman who loves the traditions and good name of his race has ample reason to find fault, for not only is every allusion to the people of Ireland very offensive, but all emigrants from that country to this, prior to the Revolution, no matter of what branch of the race, Irish or Scotch, are claimed by and credited to the latter. " In morals, blood, language and religion," they, the "Scotch-Irish," were different from the Irish, it is said. The intelligent reader can see for himself how false this statement is, so far as the blood and language are concerned ; and as for the morals of the Irish people, let an unprejudiced writer decide.

Sir Henry Maine, in his " History of Institutions," "Brehon Laws," page 80, says: — " At the present moment Ireland is probably that one of all western countries in which the relation of the sexes are most nearly on the footing required by the Christian theory. Nor is there any reasonable doubt that this result has been brought about in the main by the Roman Catholic clergy." So much for the morals of the Irish people in 1875 ; and in this they are in accord with those of their ancestors at the period written of by Morrison and Cochrane, according to the testimony of Lecky on " European Morals." If the morals of the Scotch colonists in Ireland in 1620 differed from those of their Irish cousins, it would not be to the discredit of the latter.

A short study of the work of Maine quoted will satisfy

the writers mentioned of the origin of the Scots, as he con-
stantly alludes to the Celts of Ireland and of the Scottish
Highlands, to the "Newer Scotia," and to the "Scots of
Ireland." On page 80 he says:—"It cannot be doubted,
I think, that the primitive notion of kinship, as the cement
binding communities together, survived longer among the
Celts of Ireland and the Scottish Highlands than in any
western society." Prejudice has for centuries prevented
English scholars from studying the early history of Ireland, but, thanks to the efforts of writers like Maine, this
is now being done. He alludes to this prejudice when he
writes:—There was no set of communities which, until
recently, supplied us with information less in amount and
apparent value concerning the early history of law than
those of Celtic origin.

This was the more remarkable because one particular
group of small Celtic societies, which have engrossed more
than their share of the interest of the country—the clans
of the Scottish Highlands—had admittedly retained many
of the characteristics, and in particular the political char-
icteristics, of a more ancient condition of the world almost
down to our own day. But the explanation is that all
Celtic societies were, until recently, seen by those com-
petent to observe them through a peculiarly deceptive
medium. A thick mist of feudal law hid the ancient
constitution of Irish society from English observation.
"The group of Irish scholars, distinguished by a remarkable sobriety of thought, which has succeeded a school almost infamous for the unchastened license of its specula-
tions on history and philology, has pointed out many things
in Irish custom which connected it with the Archaic prac-
tices known to be still followed or to have been followed
by the Germanic races."

Of the piety of the Irish people of the fourteenth century, the following from Maine, page 17, bears proof: "One MS., the 'Senachus Mor,' or the great Book of Laws, known to be as old at least as the fourteenth century, has written on it a touching note by a member of the family to whom it belonged: 'One thousand three hundred two and forty years from the birth of Christ till this night; and this is the second year since the coming of the plague into Ireland. I have written this in the twentieth year of my age. I am Hugh, son of Conor McEgan, and whoever reads it let him offer a prayer of mercy for my soul. This is Christmas night, and on this night I place myself under the protection of the King of Heaven and Earth, beseeching that he will bring me and my friends safe through the plague.' " Hugh wrote this in his own father's book in the year of the great plague. Again, on page 237, he speaks of "Iona or Hy as the religious house founded by St. Columba near the coast of the 'newer Scota.' "

The failings of the "Scotch-Irish," in the way of a love of whiskey, festivities at weddings, the observance of wakes, and an occasional bout with the shillalagh, are charged to their Irish neighbors, from whom they contracted these bad habits. The love for the ardent is still a Scotch failing; its praises have been sung by "Bobbie" Burns and Sir Walter Scott, both of whom dearly loved the "Mountain Dew," and the refrain has been chanted in our own day by no less a person than Professor Blackie; but in view of the fact that all in those times "took their tod"—Catholic, Puritan, or Presbyterian—whiskey, New England rum, or hard cider, according to their liking—it would be a waste of time to endeavor to refute such charges, especially when history informs us that neither church, schoolhouse, nor barn, in New Hampshire, could be raised or dedicated without a liberal supply of New England rum. Instead of casting reflections, one ought to be thankful that such things would be simply impossible in our own day, and that the fault was not of the people, but of the times in which they lived.

This fear on the part of so many, who pride themselves on their descent from the settlers of Londonderry, N. H., of being confounded with the modern Irish, can easily be inferred. The heavy migration of the latter day Irish, mainly of the Catholic faith, and principally from the south, east, and west of Ireland, began about the year 1840. They were poor, ignorant of letters as a rule, and their manners, customs and speech strange to those to "the manner born." Thousands came here without mothers, wives, or sisters, and with no chance to practice their religion, or, at least, to have an opportunity to have its tenets expounded. For their lack of education they were not responsible, nor for their poverty;—the former they were deprived of for 150 years by legal enactment; the latter was the natural effect of the laws under which the settlers of Londonderry could not live, and from which they fled 121 years before. But these modern Celts brought with them what the country needed,—strong, muscular bodies, clear heads, willing hands to work, clean hearts, and honest purposes; and when the hour finally arrived, and their wives and children were gathered around them, new homes and new firesides were founded, the "Soggarth aroon" followed, and the modest little chapel arose, crowned with the sacred symbol of Calvary—the cross—to be followed by the many beautiful churches and stately cathedrals, tributes to their piety, devotion and self-sacrifice.

And when the world had seen the tireless labor bestowed by these Irish on the railroads, on the canals, on the wharves, and in the mines, their stern loyalty and unflinching bravery on the battle-fields of the War for the Union, and the steady advance in all the walks of life,—commercial and mercantile, the army and navy, the law and the church, —of those of the first generation following, their bitterest enemies were compelled to acknowledge that they were true kin of the people whose piety, vigor and learning astonished Europe from the sixth to the tenth centuries, and gallant kindred of the heroes who made the Irish brigade of France a terror to its enemies and a glory to the race from which it sprang.

It was then but natural that the descendants of those whom tyranny had driven from Ireland early in the eighteenth century, educated by their surroundings, and prejudiced against them through their teachings, should regard the new comers with aversion, and dread to own them as kindred. But the advance made by those emigrants and their children in our own day, and a knowledge of the early history of the race, will remove this prejudice, and in time make them as proud of their origin as those who have sprung direct from the cradle of the Scots—Ireland, the original Scotland of history.

It is the supposition of many writers that all the old Irish are Catholic, and the later stock Protestant. While this may be true in the main, there are, nevertheless, good sized minorities of the former Protestant, and of the latter Catholic, as their names indicate. The founders of Methodism in America came here direct from Ireland, and while Philip Embury may have been of German origin, among the pioneers the names of John Finnegan, Joseph Mitchel, Henry Ryan, and Peter Moriarty, which appear on the pages of Rev. Dr. Abel Stevens's "Memorials of the Introduction of Methodism in the Eastern States," about the period of 1790, are fully as Irish in appearance as the names of Chaplain McCabe or Dr. John Lanahan of the Methodist Church South in our own day. A study of modern Irish history would verify this statement. The lineal descendant

of Brian Boru, the hero of Clontarf, is an Episcopalian,—
O'Brien, Earl of Inchiquin; and a direct shoot of Dermot
MacMurrough, of infamous memory, is one of the staunch-
est supporters of the same church. Both are as anti-Irish
as the most belligerent Englishman, while, on the other
hand, some of the purest patriots and most devout Irish
Catholics were of English or German stock.

Of the ancient art and learning of Ireland, English and
Scotch bear witness. Pinkerton, a noted Scottish writer,
who has already been quoted, speaks of the Life of St.
Columbkille "as being the most complete piece of ancient
biography that all Europe can boast of." It was written by
St. Adamnanus, Abbot of Iona, who died in 703. Like
Columba, he was an Irishman, and a successor of the saint
as Abbot of Hy. This opinion of Pinkerton's is endorsed
by David McPherson's "Annals of Commerce," Edin.,
1805. This gentleman made copious extracts from the
works of Adamnanus, all of which show a high state of
Irish civilization as early as the fifth and sixth centuries,
facts which will stagger the belief of our modern defamers.

From Adamnanus, Mr. McPherson proves "that the
arts, conducive not only to the conveniences but to the
luxury of life, were known and practised to an excess in
Ireland in the fourth, fifth, and sixth centuries; that the
luxury of riding in chariots was common; that the bodies
of the dead, at least those of eminent rank, were enveloped
in fine linen; that though ale was a common beverage, wine
was also used; that in churches bells were used; that they
had long vessels in which they performed extended voyages
of fourteen days into the Northern ocean; that they had instruments and trinkets of gold, belonging to ages antecedent
to authentic history. As civilized countries do not carry the
precious metal into countries in an inferior state of civilization, it seems more probable, says Mr. McPherson, that the

gold was found in the mines, of which there are still many traces in Ireland, than that it was imported there. "We should suppose, with Tacitus, that Ireland had a greater foreign trade than Great Britain.

"The first mention of Ireland in ancient times occurs in a poem by Orpheus, where he speaks of it as Iernis, 500 years before Christ. To the Romans it was known as Hibernia, and to the Greeks as Ivernia and Ierne. Aristotle speaks of two islands 'situated in the ocean beyond the Pillars of Hercules, called Britannic Albion and Ierne, beyond the Celtae.' 'Pomponious Mela, with quite an Irish warmth of eulogy, declares the herbage to be so luxuriant that the cattle who feed on it sometimes burst.' Pliny repeats this statement, and adds, 'that the Hibernian mother trains her child from the first to eat food from the point of a sword.' But the most important of all is Ptolemy, who describes the country, and gives the names of the principal rivers, promontories, seaports, and inland towns. Diodorus Siculus mentions it, and wrote 'that the Phoenicians, from the very remotest times, made repeated voyages for commerce.'"

The writer of the article, in Rees's Cyclopedia, on Ireland says,—"It does not appear improbable, much less absurd, to suppose that the Phoenicians might have colonized Ireland at an early period, and introduced their laws, customs, and knowledge, with a comparatively high state of civilization." Tacitus, referring to a proposed invasion of Ireland under the direction of Agricola, says,—"In the fifth year of these expeditions, Agricola, passing over in the first ship, subdued in frequent victories nations hitherto unknown. He stationed troops along that part of Britain which looks to Ireland, more on account of hope than fear, since Ireland, from its situation between Britain and Spain, and opening to the Gallic sea, might well connect the most powerful parts of the empire with reciprocal advantage. Its extent, compared with Britain, is narrower, but exceeds that of any islands in our sea. The genius and habits of the people, and the soil and climate, do not differ much from those of Britain. Its channels and ports are better known to commerce and merchants. Agricola gave his protection to one of its petty kings, who had been expelled by faction, and with a show of friendship retained him for his own purposes. I have often heard him say that Ireland could be conquered and taken with one legion and a small reserve; and such a measure would have its advantages as regards Britain, if Roman power were extended on every side, and liberty taken away as it were from the latter island."

The island was never conquered or even explored by the Romans. Sir John Davies remarked, regarding the boast of Agricola, that "if he had attempted the conquest thereof with a larger army, he would have found himself deceived in his conjecture." And William of Newburgh has also remarked that "though the Romans harassed the Britons for three centuries after this event, Ireland never was invaded by them. The Scots and Picts gave their legions quite sufficient occupation defending the ramparts of Adrian and Antoninus, to deter them from attempting to obtain more, when they could hardly hold what they already possessed."

Of the truth of the quotations from the writers mentioned, modern thought and research are bearing proof; and the time has arrived, thanks to writers and philologists like Max Muller, when statements referring to the ancient civilization of Ireland will not be received with a look of contemptuous doubt, or a sneer of scornful incredulity.

Of ancient Irish art, a writer in Chambers says,—"Of articles of metal, stone, clay, and other materials in use among the ancient Irish, a large collection has been formed in the Museum of the Royal Irish Academy in Dublin. It is remarkable that a greater number and variety of antique golden articles of remote age have been found in Ireland than in any other part of northern Europe, and the majority of the gold antiquities illustrative of British history now preserved in the British Museum are Irish."

Speaking on the same subject, Prof. Llewellen Jewitt, F. S. A., in the Art Journal, Appleton's reprint, remarks,— "The Irish, as we all know, were in ancient times—as many of the gifted sons and daughters of that gifted land are at the present day—remarkable for the beauty and intricacy of their designs, and for the marvellous delicacy, precision, and finish in their workmanship, whether in metal, stone, or vellum. Their early designs present remarkable and striking peculiarities, and exhibit a greater inventive power, a stricter adhesion to sound principles of art, than those of any other contemporaneous people. The style, which can only be called the 'Irish style,' is national to that country, and was pursued for many centuries with the same spirited characteristics, and the same amount of elaboration and intricacy. The carved stone crosses, the metal fibule, shrines, bells, cases, croziers, illuminated manuscripts, and indeed every species of ornamental work, evince the same skill in design and the same general adhesion to one fixed principle, and show that whatever the material worked upon, or whatever the size or use of the object upon which that work was expended, the mind of the Irish artist was guided by the same feeling and the same fixed idea."

In the illustrated catalogue of the Archaeological Museum at Edinburgh, 1856, is a description of St. Patrick's bell: "It is six inches high, five inches broad, and four inches deep, and is kept in a case or shrine of brass, enriched with gems and with gold filigree."

Of the objects of antique art in gold, brooches especially, found in Ireland, the writer says,—"Many are wonderfully beautiful in workmanship, and still more so in design, and it is doubtful if antiquity has left us anything more perfect in the way of personal ornament than the so-called Hunterstone brooch. It was found in 1830 in the parish of Kilbride, Ayrshire; it has a legible inscription in Gaelic."

One of the first specimens of cinerary urns found in the British Isles was discovered in a small stone chamber in Bagenalstown, County Carlow, Ireland, and is now in the Museum of the Royal Irish Academy in Dublin. Of this branch of early Irish art Prof. Jewitt treats exhaustively, and illustrates with many engravings. Of urns found in different parts of Ireland he says,—"It is not too much to say that in an equal degree with metal work, with illuminations, and with interlaced designs in sculpture, the decorations, nay, even the general forms, of the early fictile productions of the Irish people are in advance of those of coeval nations, and exhibit more 'flow' and general taste than they do."

Charles G. Leland, director of the industrial art schools of Philadelphia, in an interesting article in Longman's Magazine for November, 1886, on ancient Irish art, says,—"It is possible that the mere suggestion of industrial art finding an opening for the unemployed in Ireland will bring a smile to many who should give it serious consideration, and who possibly anticipate something funny to say at Irish expense. And yet the Irishman has capacity for art. It was a clever race in prehistoric times, and no one can say the stream was ever less broad than it is now. It had men who were almost Shakespeares, and who were quite as much as Bopps and Grimms, before we had writing. Now if I can prove that there ever was a time when the Irish were pre-eminently an art-loving and artistic people, I shall beg leave to assume, that, arguing from the strongest analogy, they may again become so. It is only within a few years that one could venture such a statement: until very recently the world was not well enough educated to understand it. We are only just coming into an age when decoration is deemed to be an art at all. To the connoisseur dilittante of the last generation, nurtured in the renaissance and in statue life, the wondrous 'Book of Kells,' that triumph of a pure, illuminated manuscript, seemed an eccentric barbarism and an industrious idleness.

"And I have yet to hear or read anywhere, what I earnestly believe, that the so-called later Celtic, or purely Irish, decoration is, take it altogether, the most elegant and ingenious style of decoration which the world has ever seen. When Roman art had died, and was not yet fully revived in the Romanesque, there sprang up in an obscure part of Europe that which eventually gave tone to, and determined more than any cause whatever, the decorative art of the middle age. When I say the decorative art of this period, I say, in a word, all its art, for there never was a phase of art more decorative. It compared to the classic or the Greek, as a forest of one kind of tree, bound with a million vines and colored with millions of flowers, compares with a group of ferns, or of a single grove of palms. Now the soul of all this fanciful tracery and wild ornament was derived from the illuminations of the manuscripts. This art preceded the wonderfully florid architecture in which it re-appeared, and this art was Irish. It was purely and entirely Irish. In the darkest day of the dark ages, there was a bright fire of intellect in Ireland. It attested itself, not only in the purest piety, in theology and poetry, in legend and lay, but in a new art. From this fire went bright sparks, which kindled fresher fires all over Europe.

"Irish monks carried to the court of Charlemagne the new style of illuminating manuscripts, and combined it with heavy Romanesque, which was yet almost Roman. From this union sprang the new art, but all that was most original and remarkable in it was Irish. Those who would verify what I have said, for examples of it may consult the 'Palaeographia' of Westwood, who was one of the first, I believe, to make known the wonderful influence which Ireland exerted in art. Architecture, also, flourished in Ireland, at this time, to a degree which is even known now to but few. I hazard the statement, which will, I believe, yet be verified, that before the advent of Norman architecture there were more and better stone edifices than were erected by the Saxons.

"To the impartial student of decorative art, the later Celtic metal-work is almost miraculous. Its two great differences from the contemporary ornament of Europe, or what came later, lie in this. Gothic art, with all its richness and variety, was given to repetition. Later Celtic is simply of incredible variety: every design in it indicates that its artists never repeated themselves. They combined intricacy with elegance to a degree which astonishes us. Whatever opinion the world may have as to the esthetic value of Irish art, one thing is true: the men who made it had the minds which could have mastered anything in the decorative art, for they were nothing if they were not original, and their art was manifestly universal or general. It was produced by common artisans. It was of the people. It was most evidently not produced under the greatest advantages of wealth and luxury or patronage. I do not, and cannot believe, that, the blood being the same with that of the men who a thousand years ago taught decorative art to all Europe, the Irish of the present day cannot do what they did of old."

In all the quotations made thus far, not one has been taken from Irish writers. The day has not yet arrived when Irish authority can be offered with the full assurance that it would be accepted. Prejudice and ignorance, as the last writer alludes to, still control the pen and the voice of many who would, were it otherwise, be the loudest in defence of the Niobe of nations; but it will come in its own good time. Meanwhile, with such a record before them, can the modern "Scotch-Irish-American" be ashamed of such an ancestry?

Hon. William Parsons, the celebrated lecturer, a relative of the illustrious Lawrence Parsons, Earl of Rosse, an Irish Protestant, and a lover of his country, in an article recently published, voices the sentiment of the true Irishman, when, speaking of the battle of Clontarf, where the power of the Northmen was forever broken in Ireland, says,— "Yet this was once the arena of a bloody battle which decided the fate of a kingdom. The struggle took place at this spot, where an Irish prince met and repelled the Danish invaders—the terror of Europe and of imperial Rome itself. Here the galleys of the Norsemen anchored; here stands the old castle built by the Crusaders; here the well where the victor slacked his thirst, and which to-day bears his name. But the dust of antiquity, like that of Egypt, has fallen heavily upon a spot rich in historical associations. If the stranger inquires of an inhabitant for any particulars, the reply is a crude one,—'Yes, here took place the battle of Clontarf,' the Salamis of Ireland. That is all that is known, for this anomalous island has no history. All records of historic fame lie in musty archives of the state. All deeds of enterprise and chivalry, to remind posterity of the prowess and glory of their forefathers, are forbidden and put down by an act of parliament: not an Irish history permitted in an Irish national school. 'That man is little to be envied whose patriotism would not gain force upon the plains of Marathon, or whose piety would not grow warmer amid the ruins of Iona,' are the words of Doctor Johnson, speaking of the value of history, and are good illustrations of historic Grecian valor and ancient Irish Christianity. The Greeks at Marathon were more successful in contending with their foes, the Persians, than the unarmed, peaceful monks of Iona, whose lives and works were destroyed by the accursed, much vaunted Vikings, the scourge of religion and morality. Doctor Johnson, writing on a proposal to compile a national history of Ireland in his day, said,— 'Such a design should be prosecuted. Ireland is less known than any other country as to its ancient state. I have long wished that the Irish literature were cultivated. Ireland is known by tradition to have been the seat of piety and learning, and surely it would be very acceptable to all those who are curious, either in the origin of nations or the affinities of language, to be further informed of the resolutions of a people so ancient and once so illustrious.' "

In the article on the "Welsh Language and Literature," in Chambers' Encyclopaedia,* it is stated "that preposterous as the views of most patriotic Welshmen are on this subject—antiquity of their language—it is undoubtedly true that the Welsh is one of the oldest living languages in Europe, and that it possesses a literature reaching back to remoter times than that of any modern tongue except Irish." From a sketch of the "Life of St. Willibrod," in the same work, it can be found that this "saint, apostle of the Frisians, and first bishop of Utrecht, was born in the kingdom of Northumbria in 658; educated in the monastery of Ripon; and for final instruction was sent, like most of the monks of that age, to Ireland, where he remained thirteen years."

Chambers (vol. i, p. 432), speaking of the Isles of Arran, near the entrance of Galway bay, says,—"Anciently these islands formed an important ecclesiastical seat. Containing at one time twenty churches and monasteries, Irish-

*The edition of Chambers· quoted throughout this work is that of London and Edinburgh, 1868.

more was the centre of these, still known as 'Arran of the Saints.' " Many pilgrims still visit the old shrines and relics scattered through the islands. St. Kenanach's church, built in the seventh century, still exists, as well as the stone oratories and little bee-hive stone huts of the monks of the sixth and seventh centuries. The military antiquities are not less remarkable, consisting of nine circular Cyclopean fortresses of unhewn, uncemented stone, portions of the walls still being twenty feet high. The largest of these, Dun Angus,— Fort of Angus,—on a cliff 220 feet high, is one of the most magnificent barbaric monuments in Europe. On page 662, vol. 1, Chambers', there is this mention of Bangor abbey (Ban-choir), the white choir, one of the most noted seats of learning in Europe between the seventh and the tenth centuries: "St. Cungall founded Bangor abbey in 555, of which the ruins still remain. From this abbey, Alfred selected professors when he founded the University of Oxford. In the ninth century it contained three thousand inmates." It was situated near the entrance to Belfast lough. Of Cashel, another celebrated seat of learning in ancient times, in the south of Ireland, the same authority (vol. ii, p. 648) speaks: "The ancient kings of Munster resided there. The top of the heights, or 'rock of Cashel,' is occupied by an assemblage of the most remarkable ruins in Ireland. The ruins consist of a cathedral founded in 1169; a stone-roofed chapel, built in 1127 by Cormac MacCarthy, king of Munster, and the most perfect specimen of the kind in the country; Hore abbey, founded in 1260; the palace of the Munster kings; and a round tower ninety feet high and fifty-six feet in circumference."

Of St. Columbkille, the same authority says,—"He was one of the greatest names in the early ecclesiastical history of the British Isles; was born in Donegal. His father was connected with the princes of Ireland and the west of

Scotland. Among those with whom he studied were St. Congall, St. Ciaran, and St. Cainnech. In 546 he founded Derry. So conspicuous was his devotion, that he received the name of St. Colum-cille, or 'Columba of the Church.' In 563, in his forty-second year, he founded the celebrated school of Iona, on the west coast of Scotland, from whence went forth missionaries to the Picts, the Scots of Caledonia, the Saxons of Britain, and to the pagans of northern Europe. He died at the age of seventy-seven, between the 8th and 9th of June, 597. The Venerable Bede said of him, 'But whatever sort of person he was himself, this we know of him for certain, that he left after him successors eminent for their strict continence, divine love, and exact discipline.' His life was written by one of his successors, St. Adamnan, 679, and contains the most accurate description of the habits and customs of the Scots of those times of any work in existence."

"St. Columba, one of the most learned and eloquent of the many missionaries whom Ireland sent forth to the continent during the Dark Ages, was born in Leinster about the year 545; studied in the great monastery of Bangor, in Ulster; went to France in his forty-fifth year, with twelve companions, and founded the monasteries of Annegray, Lupenil, and Fontaine. For rebuking the vices of the Burgundian court he was expelled from France. He went to Lombardy, and founded, in 612, the famous monastery of Bobbio, in the Apennines, where he died in November, 615. His life, written within a century after his death by Jonas, one of his successors, has been repeatedly printed. The most complete edition of his works is in Fleming's Collectanea Sacra, published in Louvain in 1667, and now of such rarity that a copy sells for about $175."

He was spoken of in the highest terms by such an authority as Guizot. The town of San Columbano, in Lombardy, takes its name from the Irish monk, as the town and canton of St. Gall, in Switzerland, perpetuate the name of the most favored of his disciples. From this name of Colum, Colm, Columba, comes the modern name of MacCullum, MacCallum, McCullum-more, still common in the Highlands; and it would not be at all surprising if the ancestors of the "great admiral," Christopher Columbus, took their surname Columbo from the town named for the Irish saint eight hundred and eighty years before the discovery of America, and thus perpetuate the memory of the devout servant of God in the now glorious name of Columbia. Allegri, the celebrated Italian painter, as was the custom, took for his surname, when he acquired fame, the cognomen of Corregio from the town in which he was born; and is now known to art by that name only. It is therefore not at all improbable that the family of the great discoverer acquired their name in the same manner, and the memory of the saint and the great republic are honored alike in the poetical name of Columbia.

An abbey, founded by St. Finbar in Cork in 600, had seven hundred scholars (vol. 3, p. 242).

Of St. Gall mentioned, Chambers says that "he was a disciple of St. Columba; founded the abbey bearing his name, in the seventh century, in Switzerland; one of the distinguished band who, in that age, from the various monasteries of Ireland and the kindred establishments of Iona, carried the elements of learning and civilization over a large part of the continent of Europe. He acquired such fame for sanctity by his teaching and example, that on his death there arose, in honor of his memory, what in progress of time became one of the most celebrated of the many magnificent establishments of the Benedictine order. The succession of abbots from the days of St. Gall is carefully chronicled, and the share which each of them had in the erection and enlargement of the monastic buildings.

"Through their piety and zeal, the Abbey of St. Gall became one of the masterpieces of mediaeval architecture; and the genius and skill, which were lavished in its construction and on the decoration of its halls and cloisters, had a large share in developing the Christian art of the period. The monks of St. Gall, too, may be reckoned among the best friends and preservers of ancient literature. They were indefatigable in the collection and transcription of manuscripts, Biblical, patristic, sacred, and profane history—classical, liturgical, and legendary. Some of the manuscripts, which are still shown in the library, are monuments of the skill and industry of the copyists; and several of the classics,—Quintilian, Silius Italicus, and Ammianus Marcellinus,—have been preserved solely through the manuscripts of St. Gall."

Kind reader, pause here, and reflect. This class—the monks—you have been asked to believe were immoral, indolent, and sensual; and the race, from whence sprung the founder of this illustrious institution, to be incorrigibly ignorant, thriftless, and improvident. Think, then, on what they have done for you and for mankind, and remember that to them and to the professors of religion, the world over, whether Catholic or Protestant, the entire credit is due for the establishment of the great centres of learning, in Rome, Bangor, Cashel, Derry, Armagh, St. Gall, Oxford, Cambridge, Pavia, Bobbio, Luxeuil, Heidelburg, Dublin, Paris, Glasgow, Harvard, Yale, Dartmouth, Princeton, etc. The Voltaires, Paines, Rosseaus, and men of that ilk, have left nothing behind them but their infamous memories and their blasphemous writings; but as long as time rolls on, the pious and lasting works of the monks of the "Island of Saints" will be eternal memorials of their self-sacrifice, love, patient labors, and undying faith in the gospel taught by their Lord and Master, Jesus Christ.

For those who love to read of the labors performed by the men who turned their backs on their homes forever in order to follow in the footsteps of their Redeemer, the pages of an encyclopaedia will be dry and uninteresting, but in Montelambert's "Monks of the West" a feast awaits all who can throw bias aside, and study for themselves the story of the conversion of their ancestors to the Christian faith, by the unceasing labors and fervent faith of the disciples of Saints Patrick, Bridget, and Columbkille.

In the yard of St. Paul's Episcopal church, on Broadway, New York, and in plain view from the sidewalk, are three monuments, the most conspicuous in the cemetery, erected in memory of three men, Irish and Protestant, who would, if buried in New Hampshire, be found on the roll of illustrious "Scotch-Irishmen," but who were in life proud to be known as Irishmen, simply. One of them came here before the Revolution, a young man, an officer in the English army; served in the "old French war," resigned at its close, settled in New York state, was one of the first to draw his sword for the establishment of the Republic, one of the first four brigadiers appointed by congress, and the first of the four to die for his adopted country.

The second was a brother of one whose dying speech has been declaimed in every school-house in the land, and who barely escaped the gallows for complicity in the struggle for which his brother was hung. He was kept in prison for years, and was finally given his freedom on condition of leaving the confines of Britain. He came to New York, and, after a long and brilliant practice as an advocate, died as chancellor of the state. His death took place suddenly while in the midst of a plea, and a brass tablet, erected by the New York bar, marks the place of his death. The third, for an offence similar to that of the second, had to leave Ireland, and in the practice of his profession—that of medicine—acquired fame and renown equal to his fellow-countrymen; and the stranger, passing by on the busiest thoroughfare in the world, involuntarily pauses and pays tribute to the memories of General Richard Montgomery, Thomas Addis Emmet, and Dr. Macnevin. The inscriptions on the monuments tell the story of their deeds as well as their love of country.

In New Hampshire, as early as 1631, according to the military record, the first representative of the Emerald Isle makes his appearance in the person of "Darby Field, an Irish soldier," and one of the first to explore the White Mountains. After him in the Colonial military rolls are distinctive Irish names, long before the settlement of Londonderry, N. H., keeping up the connection until the emigration of 1719.

In vol. 1, "Provincial Papers," 1641 to 1660, are found such names as Duggan, Dermott, Gibbon, Vaughan, Neal, Patrick (minus the Kil or Fitz), Buckley, Kane, Kelly, Brian, Healey, Connor, MacMurphy, McPhaedris, Malone, Murphy, Corbett, McClary, McMullen, Martin, Pendergast, Keilly, McGowan, McGinnis, Sullivan, and Toole.

In a company commanded by Captain Gilman in 1710 are enrolled the names of Jerry Connor, Daniel Leary, John Driscoll, Cornelius Leary, Thomas Leary, Alexander McGowan, Timothy Connor, and Cornelius Driscoll. In 1724 the names of Hugh Connor, John McGowan, John Carty, Patrick Greing, Moses Connor, and John Leary appear.

To one accustomed to the given names of the Irish people, many of the foregoing will sound tolerably familiar. In the regiment commanded by Colonel Moore, at the taking of Louisburgh, Cape Breton, in 1745, are the following names enrolled: Richard Fitzgerald, Roger McMahon, John Welsh, Thomas Leary, Daniel Kelly, Daniel Welsh, Patrick Gault, Andrew Logan, James McNeil, John Logan,

Thomas Haley, John Foy, John McNeil, James McLoughlan, James McLeneehan, Nicholas Grace, Richard Kenny,
Lieut. Richard Malone, Lieut. Samuel Connor, John Mc-
Murphy, John McLoughlan, Stephen Flood, Henry Malone, Jno. Moore, Jno. Griffin, Jos. McGowan, Paul Healey,
James Moore, Wm. Kelly, Andrew McClary, Thomas Mc-
Laughlan, John McClary, David Welch, Dennis McLaughlan, Timothy Farley, James Moloney, William O. Sellaway,
Jerry Carty, and John O'Sellaway. How Sellaway came
by the O' is a puzzle to many, but it is there, and comes
from the Gaelic pronunciation of O'Sullivan, O'Suilawon.

In the war beginning at Crown Point and ending with
the invasion of Canada, 1756 to 1760, are enrolled the names
of Capt. John Moore, Samuel McDuffy, James O'Neal,
Alexander McClary, John Mitchel, John Logan, Sergt.
John Carty, Daniel Carty, Samuel Connor, John Flood,
Edward Logan, Robert McCormick, Jonathan Malone,
Patrick Strafon, James Kelly, John Kelly, Darby Kelly,
Capt. James Neal, John McMahon, Lieut. Col. John Hart,
Quartermaster Bryan McSweeny, Daniel Murphy, Daniel
Moore, James Moloney, John Ryan, James McMahon,
John Moloney, John Cunningham, Benjamin Mooney, Wil-
liam McMaster, William Ryan, Daniel Kelly, John Malone,
John McGowan, Darby Sullivan, George Madden, Edward
Welch, James Molloy, Jeremiah Carty, James McLaughlan,
John McLaughlan, Jeremiah Connor, Jonathan Conner,
John McCarrill, Capt. Hercules Mooney, Patrick Tobin,
Michael Johnson, Lieut. John McDuffy, Ensign James Mc-
Duffy, William Kelly, Patrick Clark, Patrick Donnell, Rob-
ert McKeon, John Driscoll, Daniel Driscoll, John Rowan,
Dennis Sullivan, John McClennan, Ebenezar Maloon, Dan-
iel McDuffy, John Kenny, John Connolly, John Borland,
Michael Davis, James Kelly, Joseph Moylan, John Haley,
Thomas Kennedy, Stephen McConnell, Thomas Laney,

William Clary, Samuel McConnehie, James McMurphy, James Broderick, Robert Rankin, James Connor, Samuel McGowan, Thomas Welch, Clement Grady, Patrick Maroney, John Lowd, Daniel Driscoll, John Neil, Philip Kelly, Daniel Sullivan, Levi Connor, Lieut. McMillan, John Conner, Stephen Kenny, Samuel Kenny, James Leary, Joseph Moloney, Peter Driscoll, John Ennis, Capt. James McGee, Michael Moran, Joseph McCarthy, Daniel Murphy, 2d, Valentine Sullivan, Peter Flood, John Mooney, Andrew McGrady, Major Nathan Healey, and John McGowan.

Many of these had fought nine years before at the capture of Louisburgh, and lived to take part in the War of Independence, fifteen years later. How any writer can, after looking over a list like this, claim that those who settled in New Hampshire before the Revolution, and who were called Irish, were simply the descendants of English or Scotch who had settled in Ireland, and from thence had emigrated to America, is hard to understand. The names printed here, both proper and given, are as Irish in appearance as those printed on the muster rolls of the Irish companies in the Third, Fourth, Eighth, and Tenth New Hampshire regiments of volunteers in the Civil War, as can plainly be seen on comparing them.

The names of the Starks,* McKeans, McGregors, Morrisons, McLeans, Cochranes, Nesmyths, etc., more common to Scotland, are not written with those mentioned, but on the rolls they are printed side by side, as in life those who bore them touched elbows and marched and fought in all of the skirmishes, battles, and engagements, ending only at Yorktown, and resulting in the establishment of the Re-

---

* The name, Starke, is found in Ireland as far back as the sixteenth century and at later periods. The form, Stark, also appears. The latter was borne by Palatines who settled in Ireland in 1709 or soon after. These Palatines were German Protestants of the Palatinate. In the year just mentioned, 1709, seven thousand of them were expelled by the French, under Louis XIV. Many of the exiles came to America, some located in England, and others settled in Ireland in the counties of Carlow, Limerick, Tipperary, Kerry, etc. Reference to them is made in several works, including Fitzgerald and MacGregor's *History of Ireland*.

public. But there is no doubt that careful research in Irish history will find that nearly all of these latter names have a Gaelic origin.

The Scotch MacKeans are not far removed from the Irish O'Keans. The Cochranes of the Highlands are not strangers to the Corcorans of Munster. The Morrisons of Caledonia are akin to the O'Morrisons, MacMorrisons and MacMurroughs of Ireland, and the well known Ferguson—MacFergus—is of the same name as the first Irish-Scottish king of Argyle—Fergus, crowned in 503. The O'Loughlans and McLaughlans of Connaught can find an affinity in the McLachlans of Dundee. The O'Lenaghans, modern Linehans of Limerick, can find their kindred, the Mac-Clannahans, modern Lanahans, on the banks of the Clyde. Representatives of both names are well known in this country in the persons of Dr. John Lanahan of Maryland, of the Methodist church, and Charles T. McClannahan, the well known publisher of Masonic works in New York. Whether or not Stark is an abbreviation of Starkey is a question to be settled by those who bear the name; but to the unprejudiced reader, without the slightest knowledge of the Gaelic language, the similarity can be noticed.

One of Concord's first schoolmasters, according to Dr. Bouton's history, was Patrick Guinlon. Rev. Edward Fitzgerald was pastor of the Presbyterian church, in Worcester, in 1725. Maurice Lynch was the first town clerk of Antrim, N. H., one of its most prominent citizens, and, it is recorded, a beautiful penman; Tobias Butler was an associate, also a fine scholar and born in Ireland. Capt. Henry Parkinson, soldier and teacher, born in Ireland, lived in Canterbury, N. H., was quartermaster of Stark's regiment. His epitaph, after Virgil, is cut on his tombstone, in Latin:

"Hibernia begot me, Columbia nurtured me, Nassau Hall taught me. I have fought, I have taught, I have labored with my hands."

But it is not alone in New Hampshire that men of this blood were found in those days. They were all over the thirteen colonies, meeting the same obstacles through race or religious prejudice, but overcoming them in the end. Outside of the colonies they filled high positions in Florida and Louisiana. O'Donoju in the latter, and O'Reilly in the former, have their memories preserved in the archives as royal governors of the two provinces, and no colonial ruler was held in higher esteem than the Irish Catholic Dongan, governor of New York, under the ill-fated James. From the same colony during the Revolution went forth Generals Richard Montgomery and James Clinton—one of Irish birth, the other of Irish parentage.

In Maine, the five O'Brien brothers, sons of Maurice O'Brien, from Cork, immortalized themselves by making the first capture on sea after the commencement of hostilities, and rendered solid service to the country for the seven years following. Their descendants are still noted men, ship-builders and ship-owners in the "Pine Tree State," and have kept the O' to the name for over a hundred years, when others were prone to drop it.

A representative of another of the noted old Irish families—Kavanagh—was one of Maine's governors; and a son of Governor James Sullivan of Massachusetts—the Hon. William Sullivan—was one of the founders and original proprietors of Limerick, Me., named in memory of the birthplace of his grandfather, in the south of Ireland. Charles Carroll of Carrollton, the last survivor of those who affixed their names to the immortal Declaration, Bishop John Carroll, and Daniel Carroll were good scions of the race in the colony of Maryland, the home of the "Maryland Line," on whose rolls were many of the well known old Milesian names of O'Reilly, MacMahon, O'Neill, O'Brien, etc. Thomas Lynch and Edward Rutledge of South Carolina, George Read and Thomas McKean of Delaware, Matthew Thornton of New Hampshire, Thomas Nelson of Virginia, George Taylor of Pennsylvania, and James Smith were natives of Ireland or of Irish origin.

One of the first heroes of the navy, and who is generally called its father, was Commodore John Barry, an emigrant from Wexford, Ireland. As a man, an officer, and a citizen, his character was stainless, and a perusal of his life will be an interesting study for all who love honesty in public and purity in private life.

Of the aid rendered the colonies by the Irish in the Revolution, the testimony of Joseph Galloway, a Pennsylvania tory, before the English parliament in 1779, bears witness. In answer to the question of the nativity of the army enlisted in the service of the Continental congress, he said,—"The names and places of their nativity being taken down, I can answer the question with precision. They were scarcely one-fourth natives of America,—about one-half Irish,—the other fourth English and Scotch"* (vol. xiii, page 431, British Commons Reports).

General Robertson, who had served in America twenty-four years, swore,—"I remember General Lee telling me that he believed half of the rebel army were from Ireland." (Ibid., page 303.)

In July, 1780, the Friendly Sons of St. Patrick, of Philadelphia, or twenty-seven of them, subscribed for the relief of the starving patriots at Valley Forge the sum of $103,-500. Gen. Stephen Moylan, of the dragoons, was the president of the society, and among those who paid towards the fund was George Meade, grandfather of the hero of Gettysburg. In accepting membership in this society, General Washington wrote to the president,—"I accept with singular pleasure the ensign of so worthy a fraternity as that

*From "North American Review," October, 1887.

of the Sons of St. Patrick, in this city, a society distinguished for the firm adherence of its members to the glorious cause in which we are embarked."

Again: In reply to an address of the Catholics of the United States in 1789, Washington said,—"I presume that your fellow-citizens will not forget the patriotic part which you took in the accomplishment of their revolution and the establishment of their government."

This is strong testimony to the plea that not only were there Catholic Irish here before the Revolution, but that they were here in large numbers; and that sympathy for the cause of the colonists extended to the Irish in Ireland is evident from the testimony of Governor Johnston, in the English house of commons in 1775, when he said,— "I maintain that some of the best and wisest men in the country are on the side of the Americans, and that in Ireland three to one" are on their side.

That the delegates to the Continental congress, held in Philadelphia, realized the obligation due the people of Ireland, and that they appreciated their friendship and sympathized with them in the efforts to alleviate their own sufferings, is evident from the address* issued from that body to the Irish people wherein they say,—"We are desirous, as is natural to injured innocence, of possessing the good opinion of the virtuous and humane. We are particularly desirous of furnishing you with a true state of our motives and objects, the better to enable you to judge of our conduct with accuracy, and determine the merits of the controversy with impartiality and precision."

After giving in detail the grievances under which they suffered, the monopoly of trade enjoyed and the imposition of unjust taxes by the British government, the address

---

* This address was directed "To The People of Ireland" who were greeted as "Friends and Fellow Subjects." It was signed, in behalf of the Congress, by John Hancock, President.

goes on to state that they "agreed to suspend all trade with Great Britain, Ireland, and the West Indies, hoping by this peaceable mode of opposition to obtain that justice from the British ministry which had so long been solicited in vain. And here permit us to assure you that it was with the utmost reluctance we could prevail upon ourselves to cease commercial connection with your island. Your parliament had done us no wrong, you had ever been friendly to the rights of mankind, and we acknowledge with pleasure and gratitude that your nation has produced patriots who have nobly distinguished themselves in the cause of humanity and America. On the other hand, we are not ignorant that the labor and manufactures of Ireland, like those of the silkworm, were of little moment to herself, but served only to give luxury to those who neither toil nor spin. We perceived that if we continued our commerce with you, our agreement not to import from Britain would be fruitless, and we were, therefore, compelled to adopt a measure to which nothing but absolute necessity would have reconciled us. It gave us, however, some consolation to reflect that, should it occasion much distress, the fertile regions of America would afford you a safe asylum from poverty, and, in time, from oppression also—an asylum in which many thousands of your countrymen have found hospitality, peace, and affluence, and become united to us by all the ties of consanguinity, mutual interest, and affection."

Continuing, the address in vigorous language describes the treachery, cruelty, rapacity, and cowardice of the British officials and soldiery, in a strain also familiar to readers of Irish history, the murders and bloodshed committed in Ireland by the same soldiery being repeated in New England. It closes by saying,—"Accept our most grateful acknowledgments for the friendly disposition you have always shown toward us. We know that you are not without your grievances, we sympathize with you in your distress, and are pleased to find that the design of subjugating us has persuaded the administration to dispense to Ireland some rays of ministerial sunshine. Even the tender mercies of government have long been cruel towards you. In the rich pastures of Ireland many hungry parricides have fed, and grown strong to labor in its destruction. We hope the patient abiding of the meek may not always be forgotten.

"But we should be wanting to ourselves, we should be perfidious to posterity, we should be unworthy that ancestry from which we derive our descent, should we submit with folded arms to military butchery and depredation to gratify the lordly ambition or sate the avarice of a British ministry. In defence of our persons and property under actual violation, we have taken up arms; when that violence shall be removed and hostilities cease on the part of the aggressors, they shall on our part also. For the achievement of this happy event we confide in the good offices of our fellow-subjects beyond the Atlantic. Of their disposition we do not yet despond, aware, as they must be, that they have nothing more to expect from the same common enemy than the humble favor of being last devoured."

How prophetic these words have proven can be seen by the millions of Irish blood in the United States to-day. America has as truly been the asylum and home of the descendants of those in Ireland to whom this address was made, over one hundred and twenty-five years ago, as it was for the thousands of their countrymen at the time it was written, and whose efforts in the War for Independence hastened the triumph of the republic. Sir Henry Maine has been quoted in regard to the morals of the Irish people, and the name of Lecky mentioned. The reader will pardon, in an article already too long, an extract from the latter.

In the "History of European Morals," vol. 1, he quotes from "Wayland's Elements of Moral Science," page 298, what will with force apply to the Irish nation: "That is always the most happy condition of a nation, and that nation is most accurately obeying the laws of our constitution, in which the number of the human race is most rapidly increasing. Now, it is certain that under the law of chastity, that is, when individuals are exclusively united to each other, the increase of population will be more rapid than under any other circumstances."

Again, in vol. 1, p. 153, he writes,—"The nearly universal custom of early marriages among the Irish peasantry has alone rendered possible that high standard of female chastity, that intense and jealous sensitiveness respecting female honor, for which, among many failings and some vices, the Irish poor have long been pre-eminent in Europe." * * *

"Had the fearful famine which in the present century desolated the land, fallen upon a people who thought more of accumulating substance than of avoiding sin, multitudes might now be living who perished by literal starvation on the dreary hills of Limerick or Skibberean."

"The example of Ireland furnishes us, however, with a remarkable instance of the manner in which the influence of a moral feeling may act beyond the circumstances that gave it birth. There is no fact in Irish history more singular than the complete and, I believe, unparalleled absence, among the Irish priesthood, of those moral scandals which in every continental country occasionally proves the danger of vows of celibacy. The unsuspected purity of the Irish priests in this respect is the more remarkable, because, the government being Protestant, there is no special inquisitorial legislature to ensure it, because of the almost unbounded influence of the clergy over their parishioners, and

also because, if any just cause of suspicion existed, in the
fierce sectarianism of Irish public opinion it would assur-
edly be magnified. Considerations of climate are inadequate
to explain this fact, but the chief cause is, I think, sufficient-
ly obvious. The habit of marrying at the first development
of the passions has produced among the peasantry, from
whom the priests for the most part have sprung, an ex-
tremely strong feeling of the iniquity of irregular sexual
indulgence which retains its power even over those who are
bound to vows of perpetual celibacy."

The tribute thus paid to the Irish priesthood of the
present day is in accord with what he writes of the missionaries of the Scotia of the sixth and tenth centuries. Vol.
2, p. 261.

"The Irish monasteries furnished the earliest and probably the most numerous laborers in the field. A great portion of the north of England was converted by the Irish
monks of Lindisfarne. The fame of St. Columbanus in
Gaul, in Germany, and in Italy, for a time even balanced
that of St. Benedict himself, and the school he founded at
Luxeuil became the great seminary for mediaeval missionaries, while the monastery he planted at Bobbio continued
to the present century. The Irish missionary, St. Gall, gave
his name to a portion of Switzerland which he had converted, and a crowd of other Irish missionaries penetrated
to the remotest forests of Germany. The movement which
began with St. Columba, in the middle of the sixth century,
was communicated to England and Gaul about a century
later. During nearly three centuries, and while Europe
had sunk into the most extreme moral, intellectual, and political degradation, a constant stream of missionaries poured
forth from the monasteries, who spread the knowledge of
the cross and the seeds of a future civilization through every
land from Lombardy to Sweden."

If more authorities are required to prove that the position taken by the writer at the outset is sound, the supply is simply inexhaustible. There is less known in this country to-day of the real history of Ireland, of her ancient civilization, and of the gallant, deathless struggles of her sons to preserve their nationality, than of the workmen in "King Solomon's Mines." And if the perusal of these pages arouses a spirit of inquiry and research, it is not improbable that the descendants of the Londonderry, N. H., settlers will gladly shatter the corner-stone of the fanciful fabric which they have so laboriously constructed. For if they cut the Irish off, they will be guilty of that crime unknown to the Romans for six hundred years from the founding of the Eternal City, and, like the poor foundling, will be forever ignorant of the author of their being.

The testimony of Lecky is that of an Irish Protestant to the virtues of his Catholic countrymen and women. His conclusions are in accord with those of Sir Henry Maine. A comparison, then, between them and their Scotch cousins. or between them and the people of any nation on the globe, so far as morals are concerned, will not bring a blush to the cheeks of the sons or daughters of the ever-faithful Gael. And this is said without a thought of reflecting on the morals of any nation under the sun.

Here, then, is evidence sufficient to prove that if, as is claimed, the Irish of New Hampshire were "Scotch-Irish" in the estimation of some writers, or "Scotch" simply, in the opinions of others like Mr. Morrison, outside of the Granite State the emigrants from Ireland called themselves Irish, were known by others as Irish. are set down in history as Irish, named their towns like their kindred in New Hampshire, after their homes in Ireland—witness Ulster and Tyrone counties. New York; Limerick, Maine; Donegal, Pennsylvania; Lynchburgh, Virginia; Murfreesborough,

Tennessee. Even New Hampshire has two counties named in honor of two men of undoubted Irish blood—Sullivan and Carroll; and each of the states bears similar testimony in the names of persons and places. Gettysburg, of historic fame, takes its name from James Gettys, a native of Ireland; and the name of another of the race, O'Hara, the Kentucky soldier-poet, is immortalized by the adoption of his well known poem, "The Bivouac of the Dead," by the government, in having the verses cast in bronze, and placed in each of the national cemeteries throughout the land.

Allen Thorndike Rice, in an article in the "North American Review," for October, 1887, says,—"In the science of government the United Kingdom has no right to exult. Seven centuries have passed since she overran and annexed Ireland, and yet the Irish of to-day hate the United Kingdom as much as did their fathers who followed the standard of Brian Boru. British statesmen and writers have hitherto excused their failures to conciliate Ireland by attributing them to the incorrigible character of the Celtic race. But the same people whom she practically drove into exile by the million,—the most ignorant and poorest of her population,—have been absorbed into the American nationality, and are not surpassed in their loyalty by the descendants of the men of the Mayflower."

According to statistics given by the Army and Navy Journal as to the nativity of the men who fought for the suppression of the Rebellion, one hundred and forty-four thousand two hundred were born in Ireland. Of the number of men serving in the Union army, natives of this country, but of Irish parentage, statistics cannot tell, as they are set down as Americans, but that the number will largely exceed those of Irish birth, all soldiers, either in the East or West, well know.

Among those who were leaders in the great struggle,

and whose names are well known by every school-boy in the nation, were the immortal Sheridan, Meade, Logan, Gilmore, Gibbon, J. F. Reynolds of Pennsylvania, Mc-Reynolds of Michigan, Smythe of Delaware, Kilpatrick, Kearney, Shields, Meagher, Corcoran, R. H. Jackson, Lawler, Mulligan, McGinnis; McNulta of Illinois, Harney and Sweeney of Missouri, Guiney and Cass of Massachusetts, Donohoe of New Hampshire, Lytle of Ohio, Geo. A. Sheridan, J. C. Sullivan, Egan, and scores of others, all of Irish blood.

It may seen needless to recall either names or events, but as Rice has alluded to it, it is well to mention the fact that even in our own day the slander that the people of the north of Ireland are superior to those of the other sections of the country is heard on the platform, or read in the magazines or newspapers, and that this assumed superiority is due solely to the nationality of the people who are, it is claimed, either of Scotch or English origin. Admitting, for argument's sake, that the people of the north were more intelligent, it would not be at all surprising: they were the favored sons of Ireland. The screws might occasionally be put on the stubborn Presbyterians, but they could give their children an education without violation of legal enactments; and some of those who were of the English Church lived off the fat of the land at the expense of the rest. But despite these advantages, it is not true that they were more thrifty, capable, honest, or moral than their less favored brethren.

It would seem, on investigation, that where the old element had half a chance it went straight to the front, and in other countries, relieved of the load it carried in Ireland, it held its own with elements more favored by law or custom.

Within a half of a century we have seen a Nugent commander-in-chief of the Austrian army, and a Taafe premier of the empire; an O'Donnell ruling the destinies of Spain, and under his leadership its armies winning new laurels from their ancient enemies, the Moors, and a ducal coronet for their general; a MacMahon marshal of France, and president of the French republic; a Pendergast representing her most Christian majesty as governor-general of Cuba; a Lynch commander of the combined land and naval forces of Chili, and reviving in his person the glories achieved by O'Higgins, the liberator. Under the English government, those of the race who were favored by birth, who preferred place above love of country, or who were of the dominant faith, proved themselves fully equal to their more favored associates of English, Scotch, or Welsh birth, —Bourke, Lord Mayo, governor-general of the Indias; John Pope Hennessy, governor of Hong Kong; the Earl of Dufferin, governor-general of Canada; Sir Hastings Doyle, governor of Nova Scotia; Lord Wolseley, commander-in-chief of the English army; Daniel Maclise, the painter; Foley, the sculptor; Sir Charles Barry, the architect of the houses of parliament; Leech and Doyle, the artists of the London Punch; Michael Balfe and William Vincent Wallace, the operatic composers; Sullivan, of "Pinafore" fame; and many others, are among those who have won distinction in England or in her colonies.

In Ireland, O'Connell, and those who followed him, in the face of the most adverse circumstances, soon drew even from their opponents respect as well as fear, and the home of the race has no reason to grieve for the future of its sons. Parnell and his associates, O'Brien, Healey, O'Connor, Harrington, Dillon, O'Gorman, Egan, Brennan, and the balance of the noble band fighting for Home Rule, achieved the greatest moral victory that can be found in history; and this has been accomplished not alone by their patriotism, pluck, and eloquence, but by the honesty, sincerity, and purity of their lives.

In the United States the record of the race is still more marked; and among those who won imperishable honor in the War for the Union the Irish element need not take the second place. From the first Bull Run down to the day when the last shot was fired at the close of the war, Irish blood matted many a gory field, Irish valor brightened many dark hours, and the genius of sons of Irishmen turned more than one engagement from certain defeat into victory. Sheridan, the son of an emigrant from Ireland, later rose to command the army of the republic, and Rowan became second in command of the navy. Charles O'Conor, of the old historic clans of the west of Ireland, some years since stepped down from the pedestal, where he was placed by the unanimous voice of his associates of the American bar, to respond to the last call of nature.

John McCullough and Lawrence Barrett, on the American stage, in their persons revived the glories achieved by the Sheridans, Quinns, O'Neals, Powers, and scores of others in days gone by. Richard O'Gorman, Hon. James T. Brady, Judge John R. Brady, Hon. Charles P. Daly, Judge William C. Barrett, and Judge Donaghue, all of New York city, have been too well known to require but the bare mention of their names. John Lee Carroll, recently governor of Maryland, a grandson of the immortal signer, and A. P. Gorman, U. S. senator from the same state, are good types of the race in that proud old state. John Roach was removed by death from the head of the ship-builders of the nation. William Corcoran, of Washington, and Eugene Kelly, of New York, represented the race among the bankers, as Hon. William R. Grace does among the great shipping houses.

Kiernan from New York, Sewall from New Jersey, Jones of Florida, Farley of California, Kenna of West Virginia, and Mahone of Virginia, in the United States senate;

and O'Neal, Kelly, Lynch, Curtin, McAdoo, Collins, O'Donnell, MacMahon, Lawler, and Foran, in the house of representatives, are but a few of the many who have distinguished themselves in congress. Very few of those named sprung from north of Ireland stock; but the few who did would feel insulted to be called "Scotch-Irish."

From Irish stock come neither socialists nor anarchists, degeneration nor decay, physically or mentally; and the vivacity, elasticity, vigor, and strength of this old but ever young people will contribute largely to make the future American the best type of man, physical and intellectual, that has yet been produced through God's furnace from the mixture of races.

HOW THE IRISH CAME AS BUILDERS OF THE NATION.

TO the lover of history no subject can be of more interest than that treating of the origin of this republic, the development of its institutions and the gradual unification of the various races contributing to its population. One of our earliest historical writers has said that America is simply Europe transplanted, because, in the main, its people are descended from the colonists and immigrants who came here from that portion of the globe.

Washington, Lafayette, Steuben and Pulaski were noble types of the contributions of the English, the French, the German and the Polish elements, as those whose names I will mention later were fitting representatives of the land of St. Patrick.

The reputed voyages of Irish explorers to America centuries before the advent of Columbus is a subject now attracting more interest and study than ever before. Among those who have reverently considered the Irish claims in this respect may be mentioned Humboldt, Usher, Rafn, Von Tschudi, Otway, Bancroft, Butterfield, De Roo and other scholarly people. But I do not intend to dwell upon that point at this time, preferring to leave it for a future paper.

Coming down to the period of positive history, we know that Irish emigration to this country began long before the so-called "Scotch-Irish" movement to these shores —fully 75 or 100 years before. Even in New Hampshire, people bearing East, West and South of Ireland names were found as far back as 1641-1660. There is little doubt that many of these early comers were, in creed, Roman Catholics when they arrived here. It is not necessary, at this time, to discuss the anti-Catholic laws prevailing in the colonies at that and later periods. The Protestant Irish who subsequently came to these shores have, for some years past, been referred to by a certain class of writers as "Scotch-Irish." Some of these writers are manifestly biassed and deliberately ignore well known historical facts. Others are honest enough, but poorly informed on the subject.* Of late, the advocates of the shibboleth have begun to realize how ridiculous it is to call these Irish Protestants "Scotch-Irish," but forthwith proceed to make themselves still more ridiculous by calling them, instead, "pure Scotch."

In histories of New Hampshire towns colonized by emigrants from Ireland, an attempt has been made by the writers to draw a distinction between what they term the "Scotch-Irish" and the Irish. The former were, according to their theories, pure Scotch, mainly from the Lowlands, of Saxon origin, who had emigrated to Ireland, keeping themselves clear from all contact with the native Irish, from whom they differed in language, blood, morals, and religion, and from these people were sprung the founders of Londonderry, Antrim, Dublin, etc., in New Hampshire.

There is no evidence whatever to show that the original settlers held any such opinions of themselves. The first pastor, Rev. Mr. McGregor,† bore not a Lowland name,

---

* As illustrating the sympathy existing between the people of Scotia Major and Scotia Minor may be cited an important fact in connection with the battle of Clontarf. This latter event took place near Dublin, Ireland, A. D. 1014. The Irish army of about 20,000 men was commanded by Brian, the Irish monarch, then eighty-eight years of age. The Danish host approximated 21,000 men. In Brian's ranks that day valorously fought the Great Stewards of Lennox and Mar who were present with their forces from Scotland and materially contributed to the Irish victory which ensued.

† Many surnames that are commonly supposed, in the United States, to have originated in Scotland, and to be exclusively Scottish, are really of old Irish origin and were first borne in Ireland. O'Hart in his work on *Irish Pedigrees* (Fifth Edition, Vol. II. Dublin, 1892), states that the following Scotch families, among others, are of Irish origin, their

but, on the contrary, one of the proudest Highland names; and mixed with the first comers were a great many who must, from the character of their names, have been of the old Irish stock, thus proving that this theory of not mingling with the Irish has no solid foundation. The composition of the Charitable Irish Society, Boston, Mass., is perhaps the best evidence of the truth of this statement. Their names show that they were Irish of the mixed race, Irish, English, and Scotch, and from first to last considered themselves Irish, without prefix or affix.

The bulk of the English in England were Episcopalians, nearly all of the dissenters in New England were Puritans. The love existing between the Puritans and the Episcopalians was certainly no warmer than that between the Scotch Presbyterian and the Irish Catholic. It has been claimed that Scotland, especially the Lowlands, had been peopled largely by Danes and Saxons; a statement history sustains, but not to the extent as to affect either the nationality or customs of the Scots. Precisely a like condition of affairs prevailed during the same period in Ireland, the blood of the Irish people being mixed with that of the Saxons and Danes, who acquired possession before the Reformation of the greater part of the seacoast of Ireland, with the addition of the French Norman blood, very little of which mingled with that of the people of Scotland, so that it can be said, excepting the Normans, the mixture of bloods was the same in the two countries.

Writers addicted to the cant term, "Scotch-Irish," would have us believe that the native Irish were all driven out of the province of Ulster, at the time of the "planta-

---

ancestors at an early period having peopled Galloway and Argyle, from Ireland : Campbell, Colquhoun Lamont, MacAllister, MacArthur, MacCallum, MacCrory, MacDonald, MacDougall, MacGregor, MacLachlin, MacLean, MacNeal, MacQuary, etc. The name MacGregor has, in some instances been changed to Gregorson, (*i. e.* MacGregor — son of Gregor — Gregorson), Grierson, Grier and Greer. The Greers of Sea Park, Carrickfergus, Ireland, are descended in the male line from the Highland Clan MacAlpin (which was of Irish ancestry), and in the female line from the old Irish Clan O'Carroll, of Ely O'Carroll.

tion," and their places taken by Scotch and English, who were planted on the confiscated estates, and who kept aloof from those who had been dispossessed, not inter-marrying or associating in any way with them, and from those people were descended the Irish who began to come over here in 1718-'20, and who were only Irish in name, being the off-spring of English and Scotch, and properly known as "Scotch-Irish." This sort of reasoning on the part of the writers mentioned is simply nonsensical.

The character of the names of these people, or of many of them, illustrious in American history, could be easily de-termined by any student of philology, or of nomenclature, but fortunately there is another authority which tells a dif-ferent story of the Ulster plantation, and one which can-not be well gainsaid. In a footnote to page 90, volume 1, Reid's "History of the Presbyterian Church in Ireland," the author declares that "The extent of the forfeited lands as stated by Pynnar was about 400,000 acres; of these 100,000 were granted for church, school and corporation lands, about 60,000 were granted to the native Irish, and the remaining 240,000 were disposed of to the British undertakers or col-onists, the majority of whose tenants were also Irish, the original inhabitants of Ulster. These facts it is necessary to bear in mind, as Roman Catholic, and sometimes Protes-tant writers, represent the forfeited lands as comprising the whole of the six counties, and speak of the colonization of Ulster as having dispossessed and displaced the entire native population of the province." If Reid gives the cor-rect figures, and there is no reason to doubt it, the popula-tion of Ulster after the planting differed but little except in religion from that of the other parts of Ireland. There is every reason to believe that many of the native Irish be-came, in time, Presbyterians, being deprived by law of the ministrations of their own religion, and surrounded by every influence hostile to the faith of their fathers.

It is a well known historical fact that the Normans, Saxons, Danes, Germans and Huguenots, who had been colonized in Ireland, became in time, as the saying goes, more Irish than the Irish themselves, and for this, the English government was almost wholly responsible. The first generation of these people born in Ireland were treated no better than the Irish, and the result was, all united against the common enemy, England. At various periods in its history, and in many rebellions that have taken place since the Norman conquest, none have fought harder or suffered more under the English government than this mixed race, which had, as a rule, more property to plunder than the older stock, who had been despoiled of their ancestral acres generations before.

About the first arrival of these people in New England in any considerable numbers was in 1718, when over 100 families came to Boston, Mass. Of these a few went to Worcester, but were looked upon with disfavor by the residents of that town, and when ten years later a Presbyterian church was erected it was torn down in the night by the Congregationalists, and not a stick of timber was to be found the next morning. Being Irish, they were looked upon in the same light as the Irish Catholics were many years later.

A second party went to Falmouth, Me., remaining over winter. They were in a destitute condition, and an appropriation was made for their relief by the general court, which styled them the "poor Irish." The following year they came to New Hampshire, and founded the town of Londonderry,* and for a long time they were annoyed and

* Londonderry, Ireland, from which Londonderry, N. H., takes its name, was bestowed, at the time of the Plantation of Ulster, upon twelve London Companies or Guilds, i. e. the Mercers, Grocers (in part), Drapers, Fishmongers, Goldsmiths, Skinners, Clothworkers, Merchant Tailors, Haberdashers, Salters, Ironmongers, and Vintners. The district thus set apart included four baronies, of which three had constituted the old county of Coleraine. From these and other sections was evolved the present county of Londonderry, within which is the city of the name. This district became known as the "Londoners' Plantation."

persecuted by the English settlers of Haverhill, Mass., and it was not until they were found useful as Indian fighters that the persecution ceased, though the prejudice against them on account of their nationality lasted for years.

Every mention of these people in the early history of New Hampshire styles them "Irish," and there was good reason for it, for there was not a typical name representing the old Gaelic or Norman Irish that cannot be found in the Irish settlements of that day, and they are as common now in New Hampshire and in other states among the descendants of the first immigrants as they are in Ireland. From 1718 to the outbreak of the revolution the Irish had increased so rapidly that Londonderry, the parent settlement, was the most populous town in the colony, and all the new towns settled by them were thrifty and progressive.

The London Spectator said New England was uncongenial to these "Puritan Irish," but in no state of the Union has the element left its mark so indelibly as in New Hampshire, the descendants of the "Puritan Irish" filling the highest positions in the state and the nation. A glance at the pages of the provincial records and of the revolutionary rolls of New Hampshire will surprise many of those

Speaking of the city of Derry, a recent writer says: "The old town at the mouth of the Foyle is a good deal now talked of, and people appear doubtful whether to call it Derry, Londonderry or the 'Maiden City.' In the very old times, when there was no town to be christened that area now included within the walls was surrounded by the river and densely covered by oaks. An oak tree wood or forest is called in Irish *doire*, and hence the name Derry, the old Irish original name. In the sixth century St. Columbkille founded an abbey in the place, and this formed the commencement of the town which grew up round the abbey. The church attached to the abbey for the use of the public was called *teamful mor*, the great church, and hence the name of the parish in which the city is situated is still called Templemore. About the ninth century the place was called, in memory of the great founder of the abbey and town, Derry Columbkille, and this was its name for several hundred years.

In the beginning of the seventeenth century a body of English colonists, principally from London, were sent to settle in the district. They received their very liberal charter of rights in 1613, and it was then that we first find the place called London-derry. During the Civil War of 1641 the Roundheads held the city against the Royalists or Stuarts, who failed to take it. And in 1689 the Williamites held it against James II. The prefix "London" was allowed to drop even by the first descendents of the London colonists themselves, but may be used of course by anyone who is proud of the Londonizing of the place. Derry is the correct name, therefore, and indeed there are few Derrymen who call it by any other name."

Rev. James MacSparran, an Irish Protestant clergyman of Rhode Island, writing in 1752 and referring to the New Hampshire settlement says: "In this province lies that town called London-Derry, all Irish, and famed for industry and riches."

writers who are so fond of denying to the Irish any credit for what is due them for their services during the periods named, but the names are there, speaking for themselves.

The fact that a Masonic lodge was early instituted at Portsmouth, N. H., and named in honor of Ireland's patron saint, as well as that Stark's rangers, on one occasion, demanded an extra ration of grog in order to celebrate St. Patrick's day properly, proves that the customs and traditions of the old land were still kept up, more than a generation after the "Puritan Irish" made their appearance in the province.

The greater part of the families mentioned remained in Boston, and in 1730 built what is called the Presbyterian Church of Long Lane. The first pastor of this church was Rev. John Moorehead. Seven years later, on the 17th of March, 1737, twenty-six of the "Puritan Irish" remaining in Boston, all members of this church, met, and, like their countrymen in New Hampshire, celebrated St. Patrick's day. Organizing a benevolent association, they named it the "Irish Society," better known now as the Charitable Irish Society. Every name of the twenty-six original members were of the same character as those in the Londonderry settlement in New Hampshire, among them being the father and two uncles of Gen. Henry Knox;[*] the general and his son were afterwards members.

Irishmen of Scotch, English and old Irish descent, as the names denote, are borne on the rolls of the society from the first, but no man was eligible for membership unless he was born in Ireland or in some part of the British dominion, of Irish parentage. This is most conclusive evidence that these men considered themselves Irish. No Scotchman

---

[*] Knox,—A name derived from an old Irish source. In the Irish Parliament, 1797, were four bearers of the name. Two of them were in the House of Lords and two in the Commons. The former were the Bishop of Killaloe and Viscount Northland. The two in the Irish House of Commons were Hon. George Knox and Hon. Thomas Knox. Gen. Henry Knox of the American Revolution was not only a member of the Charitable Irish Society, Boston, but also of the Friendly Sons of St. Patrick, of Philadelphia.

could be admitted to membership, and the seal of the society bore the arms, not of Scotland, but of Ireland. Rev. John Moorehead, the first pastor of the Presbyterian church, was among the earlier members.

To this association belonged the principal Irish residents of Boston, and an index to the friendly feeling always existing in that place between the Catholics and Protestants of Irish origin is the fact that for over 100 years a clergyman of both churches has been the guest of the society at each anniversary. When Gen. John McNeil, one of the descendants of the Londonderry colony, was collector of Boston, in 1830, he was admitted to membership, and when President Andrew Jackson* visited Boston, in 1833, he was greeted by the society, and in response to the address of welcome, he said: "I feel grateful, sir, at this testimony of respect shown me by the Charitable Irish Society of this city. It is with great pleasure that I see so many of the countrymen of my father assembled on this occasion. I have always been proud of my ancestry and of being descended from that noble race."

Of the eighty-three soldiers holding the commissions of major or brigadier generals in the Continental army at least nineteen were born in Ireland or in America of Irish parentage. Their names and rank were Major Generals John Sullivan, Richard Montgomery, Henry Knox and Thomas Conway (Conway and Montgomery were born in Ireland), and Brigadier Generals Edward Hand, Andrew Lewis, John Armstrong, Stephen Moylan, William Irvine, John Hogan, William Maxwell, William Thompson, George Clinton, James Moore, Anthony Wayne, James Clinton, Daniel Morgan, Joseph Reed and Roche de Fermoy. Of these fifteen, nine were born in Ireland. The character of

---

* Jackson was a member of the Hibernian Society, Philadelphia, joining the organization in 1819. His membership certificate is still in existence.

the names denotes the mixture of races, but from the fact that the greater part belonged to the Friendly Sons of St. Patrick and the Hibernian Society of Philadelphia it is quite clear that they considered themselves plain Irish, without the prefix so beloved by the anti-Irish writers.

Among the governors of Irish birth, or of Irish origin, during the colonial or revolutionary periods were David Dunbar and John Sullivan of New Hampshire; Thomas Dongan and George Clinton of New York; James Sullivan of Massachusetts; John Houston, John Martin and Peter Early of Georgia; John McKinley, Thomas Collins, John Collins and Joseph Haslett of Delaware; John Hart of Maryland; James Logan, George Bryan, William Moore, Joseph Reed and Thomas McKean* of Pennsylvania, James Moore, John Rutledge and Edward Rutledge of South Carolina; Matthew Rowan and Thomas Burke of North Carolina, and William Welsh and William Patterson of New Jersey.

Among those of the same stock who have been governors of states since 1800 were John Murphy, Gabriel Moore, Hugh McVay, Benjamin Fitzpatrick, Andrew B. Moore and Edward O'Neal of Alabama; John A. Gurly and Richard McCormick of Arizona; James S. Conway, John S. Roane, Harris Flannegan and Isaac Murphy of Arkansas; Stephen W. Kearney, John G. Downey and Bennet Riley of California; Joseph Haslett of Delaware; Wilson S. Shannon, John W. Geary and Thomas Carney of Kansas; John Adair of Kentucky; Edward Kavanagh and Selden Connor of Maine; Daniel Martin, T. K. Carroll and John Lee Carroll of Maryland; Benjamin F. Butler and Thomas Talbot of Massachusetts; John S. Barry of Michigan; Willis A. Gorman and A. P. McGill of Minnesota; Charles Lynch

* A signer of the Declaration of Independence; first President of the Hibernian Society, of Philadelphia.

and William L. Sharkey of Mississippi; Thomas Francis
Meagher of Montana; William O. Butler and David Butler
of Nebraska; Stephen W. Kearney and Henry Connolly of
New Mexico; Reuben E. Fenton of New York; Wilson
Shannon and Thomas L. Young of Ohio; William Findlay,
James Pollock, Andrew G. Curtin and John W. Geary of
Pennsylvania, George McDuffee, Pierce M. Butler, Patrick
Noble, B. K. Hannegan, William Aiken, A. G. McGrath
and James L. Orr of South Carolina; James McKinn and
William Carroll of Tennessee.

Among the same stock in the United States senate
were William Kelley, John McKinley, Gabriel Moore and
Benjamin Fitzpatrick of Alabama; Solon Burland, William
S. Fulton and Stephen W. Dorsey of Arkansas; David G.
Broderick, John Conness, Cornelius Cole, Eugene Casserly
and J. T. Farley of California; James Shields of Illinois,
Minnesota and Missouri (Shields was the only man thus far
in the history of the nation to represent three separate states
in the United States senate); John A. Logan of Illinois;
Robert Hanna and Edward Hannegan of Indiana; James
Harlan of Iowa; John Adair, William F. Barry, William
Logan and John Rowan of Kentucky; Alexander Porter of
Louisiana; A. P. Gorman and Anthony Kennedy of Mary-
land; Thomas Fitzgerald and Lucius Lyon of Michigan;
James G. Fair of Nevada; William J. Sewall of New Jer-
sey; George and DeWitt Clinton, Reuben E. Fenton and
Francis L. Kernan of New York; James R. Kelley of Ore-
gon; Pierce Butler, A. B. Butler and M. C. Butler of South
Carolina; James W. Flannegan and John H. Regan of
Texas; Andrew Moore and William Mahone of Virginia.

Thirty-three years after the formation of the Irish Society of Boston seventeen persons, all of Irish birth or extraction, met at the Burns Tavern, in Philadelphia, March
17, 1771, and organized "the Society of the Friendly Sons

of St. Patrick," for friendly, social and convivial intercourse. Like the Boston Society, none but natives of Ireland or those of Irish extraction were eligible for membership. It had an honorary membership, limited to ten members at any one time. It has been often asserted and never controverted, "that no equal number of men in any of the thirteen colonies contributed more to the success of the Revolution than did the Friendly Sons of St. Patrick of Philadelphia. Nearly every member engaged in the strife, at one time or another, either on land or sea. One of them published the first daily paper in the colonies, the Pennsylvania Packet and General Advertiser. He was the first to print and publish the Declaration of Independence. A second wrote the Declaration from the first rough draft of Jefferson, and another member was the first to read it to the people from one of the windows of Independence Hall. A memorable fact, and one worthy of record, is that out of the membership of eighty-three "Sons of St. Patrick" twelve of them attained the rank of general in the War of Independence.

It is a well known fact that on the formation of parties under the administration of Washington, Jefferson, as a rule, looked to the Irish for support, and was not disappointed, as nearly all of that blood, Catholic and Protestant, followed the leadership of the author of the Declaration of Independence. Their influence was used successfully to secure the aid of the newly-arrived immigrants of their own blood; while the only way the Federalists could counteract this influence was by removing the disabilities of the hated tories, in order to secure their votes.

There was not a charge made against the Irish in the Know-Nothing campaign of 1854-5 but what was simply a repetition of what was said against the Irish of 1800, before and after the passage of the alien and sedition law, and as in

1854-55, while legislation was ostensibly aimed against all foreigners, in reality it was intended only for the Irish. So under John Adams, while the alien and sedition law was on the surface designed to affect all classes of citizens, it was enacted especially to head off the Irish; the line was not drawn between the Catholic and Presbyterian Irishmen, for all were abused indiscriminately, the familiar epithets of "bog-trotters" and "wild Irishmen" being freely applied to all.

The same cause that united the Irish in Ireland in 1798, self protection, united their kindred in America in 1800. Catholic priest and Presbyterian minister in Philadelphia stood shoulder to shoulder, opposing the passage of a law aimed, they knew, directly at their own race. The bill became a law, and the student of history is well aware of what occurred until the success of Jefferson brought about its repeal. Matthew Lyon, one of the truest types of the Irish Gael, hot-headed, brave and impulsive, was the first victim under its operation. He was a member of congress from Vermont, and for criticizing the course of the administration was fined and imprisoned. Thomas Addis Emmet was obliged to linger many weary months in an English prison, after the execution of his brother, because Rufus King, minister to England, would not give him a passport, as required by the alien law, to come to America.

At the time of this trouble John Barry was cruising off the West India Islands in command of a squadron of nine vessels. He was one of the first commodores in the American navy, a native of the county of Wexford, Ireland, and a Catholic in religion, and Matthew Lyon of Vermont was in the national house of representatives defending his native land and the men of his race from the aspersions cast on both by men of English blood. The situation was the same all over the country. The Americans of Irish blood, with few exceptions, were ardent followers of Jefferson against the federalists. In New Hampshire Gen. John Sullivan, and in Massachusetts his brother, Gov. James Sullivan, were ardent republicans.

In the colony of Georgia, as early as 1768, the colonial authorities, desiring to attract settlers to the province, passed an act to encourage immigration, appropriating the sum of £1800 for the benefit of those who availed themselves of its provisions. Under this law many Irish people came over, the government providing homes for them in the fork of Lambert creek and the great Ogeechee river. This locality was known as the "Irish settlement," and contained 270 families, nearly all Irish. Three years previous to their coming, in 1765, the name St. Patrick was given to one of four new parishes organized in the province, a proof that here were many of the same nationality in Georgia before the founding of this distinctive "Irish settlement."

In the struggle for independence these Georgia Irish, like their kindred in Pennsylvania and New Hampshire, were identified with the patriots, and among those who were active participants were men bearing the names of O'Brien, Houston, Keating, Dooley, Bryan, Gibbon, Ryan, Butler, Maxwell, Moore, Carr, etc. John Houston, son of Patrick Houston, was the first governor under the constitution, and Capt. Patrick Carr was the best known partisan fighter in the state, filling the same position in Georgia that Marion did in South Carolina.

In the colony of Virginia, before and during the revolutionary period, men bearing Irish names were prominent in military and civil life. There was hardly one of the great Gaelic names of Ireland that had not representatives in the Old Dominion, and there was not an engagement either between the settlers and the Indians, and the patriots and the

English, that the Virginia Irish were not in the forefront of the battle.

Col. John Fitzgerald was Washington's favorite aide. Maj. Connolly was in command at Fort Duquesne in 1774. Col. George Croghan was the greatest Indian trader and the most noted man of his day in the country. The defense of Fort Stephenson by his son, Maj. Croghan, is the most thrilling episode in American history. Col. Donnally has command at Greenbriar in 1781. Maj. Magill was in command of a battalion of Virginia militia before Yorktown in 1781. Maj. Lynch was in command of another battalion at the same time. Maj. William Groghan was a prisoner in the hands of the British in 1781, and begging for an exchange, in order to get back to his regiment. Capt. John O'Bannon commanded a battalion at Williamsburg in 1781. Col. Charles Lynch was one of the best-known Virginia field officers during the War of Independence. Col. Hugh McGarry was another who distinguished himself in the same contest. Col. John McElhaney, a field officer of the Continental army, was a resident of Rockbridge county in 1792, and Capt. John Brannan was in Norfolk in 1792.

Massachusetts had received, before the Revolution, a fair proportion of the Irish, for which the race has received but little credit. Up to 1640, about 21,000 immigrants in all had arrived in New England. After that date, historians say that more people moved out than into it. The addition of the Scotch, the Irish, the Acadians, who had been torn from their homes, and the French Huguenots, all prolific races, was of more moment than historians care, as a rule, to acknowledge, but an examination of the old town records will prove the truth of this statement. The chronicles of the town of Boston, Mass., are full of enactments to keep the Irish out, but it was found to be impossible. They would come despite the prejudice, for Massachusetts was the most progressive of the colonies, and these people, or many of them, being artisans, spinners, weavers, shoemakers, rope-makers, etc., their labor became welcome, and a compromise was made by obliging those of them who were well-to-do to furnish bonds for their poorer countrymen and women, to the end that they would not become public charges.

From 1635, when the name of John Kelley, who was born in England, of an Irish father, appears on the records of the town of Newbury, Mass., down to the outbreak of the War for Independence, the following names, all distinctively Irish, appear in the town records of Massachusetts, the majority being found in the early records of Boston: Kelly, Butler, O'Brien, Nolin, McCue, Mulligan, McDonnell, Murtough, Carroll, Mahoney, McMahon, McCarthy, McGowan, Hart, Donahoe, Rankin, Cogan, Kenny, Heffernan, Healey, Hayes, O'Neal, Noonan, Reardon, Griffin, Logan, Lawler, McDonough, Phelan, McGuire, Larkin, Walsh, McGee, McGlenaghan, Byrne, Copponger, Condon, Callahan, Dougherty, Daily, Fitzgerald, Farrell, Foley, Gorman, Geoghegan, Lahey, Maloney, Hogan, Cahill, Quigley, Mahoney, Feeney, Nugent, Dooley, Doyle, Lynch, Connor, McGuinness, Egan, Brady, McNamara, Connell, Mooney, Moore, Murphy, Ryan, Welch, Fitzpatrick, Connolly, Looney, Sullivan, Carney, O'Kelly, Driscoll, Keefe, Burke, Harney, Whalan, Shannan and many others.

The McCarthy family appears in the records of Boston as early as 1666, Thaddeus McCarthy being the first of the family. His son, Florence McCarthy, was one of the first men in Boston in his day, a dealer in provisions, filling a position similar to that of John P. Squire of a later day. His son, Capt. William McCarthy, was the best known ship-owner in Boston, and his son, Rev. Thaddeus McCarthy, a graduate of Harvard College, was pastor of the First Church in Worcester for thirty-seven years. He was the father of fifteen children. His brother, Capt. William McCarthy, was the quartermaster of Col. Bigelow's 15th Massachusetts regiment in the Revolutionary War, and his son, Dr. Thaddeus McCarthy, was a noted medical practitioner in Fitchburg and Keene, N. H. At the former place he had a hospital, which contained at one time 800 patients. This is a good record for one family, which cannot well be called "Scotch-Irish."

As early as 1780 and 1790, John Sullivan, Patrick Connor and Michael McCarney were associated in the manufacture of paper at Dorchester, Mass.

Michael Walsh, an Irish schoolmaster, was a teacher at Marblehead, Mass., and vicinity, in 1792, Judge Story being one of his pupils. He was the author of a "Mercantile Arithmetic" and a "New System of Bookkeeping," published in 1826.

The best known of the Irish school teachers in New Hampshire were John Suilivan, Henry Parkinson, Humphrey Sullivan, Benjamin Evans and Patrick Guinlon.

Gen. Michael Farley was one of the leading men in Ipswich, Mass., and had three sons in the Continental army. One of his townsmen was Dr. Hugh Egan, who was a well-known physician. Capt. John O'Brien, the uncle of Hon. John P. Hale of New Hampshire, one of the naval heroes of the Revolution, also receives honorable mention in the history of Newbury, and before him, in the account of the part taken by Newbury, Mass., men in the old French war, frequent mention is made of Capt. David Donohoe, who commanded an armed vessel. The diary of Lieut. Burton, published in the Revolutionary rolls of New Hampshire, mentions the appointment, as provost marshal of the army in Boston, by Washington, of Mr. William Moroney. He was a member of the Irish Society in Boston.

Captain James McGee, a president of the Boston Irish Society, was in command of a vessel wrecked in the service of the Commonwealth of Massachusetts Bay in 1778, when seventy-two of his men were lost in a great storm in mid-winter.

A certain part of the town of Sheepscott, Me., was known at Patrickstown, from the number of Irish residents. James Gowan was in Kittery in 1756. Capt. Gargill was one of Sheepscott's earliest settlers, and Rev. John Murray is mentioned in the Maine records as the man with a kind Irish heart.

Richard O'Brien, born in Maine in 1758, served in the navy during the Revolution, and for years afterward. He was captured during the Algerine war, and was a prisoner seven years. His adventures were of the most thrilling character, and after his release from captivity he was appointed by Jefferson diplomatic agent to Algiers, where he assisted Preble in his negotiations. His son, Maj. J. P. J. O'Brien, was a distinguished officer in the army.

James Kavanagh, a native of Wexford, was an extensive lumber merchant in Damariscotta in 1780. His son was president of the Maine senate, governor of Maine, member of congress and minister to Portugal. Nicholas Hearne, Fergus and Tully Higgins, Robert and William McLaughlan and Morris O'Brien and his six sons, all natives of Ireland, were residents of Scarboro, Me., in 1740-1750. Capt. John O'Brien, the oldest son of Morris, was the commander of an expedition in which his father and brothers took part, which effected the first naval capture of the Revolution. William O'Brien, one of the brothers, was captured and died in the hands of the enemy at the early age of 23. Mary O'Brien was the mother of Senator John P. Hale of New Hampshire.

John McGuire was one of the first settlers of New

Gloucester, and, as in Massachusetts, Americans of the present day in Maine bear these distinctive Irish names, the O'Briens retaining the O', which is usually discarded, and their counterparts will be found in the early history of the southwestern territories, more especially in Kentucky, where men bearing some of the best known names in Ireland have filled important stations in all walks of life. They were among the earliest pioneers, the most noted Indian fighters, eminent on the bench and at the bar, and renowned as poets, scholars and statesmen. Dr. Hart and William Coomes were among the first settlers of Harrodsburg, Ky. They came with a Catholic colony from Maryland. Collins' "History of Kentucky" credits Dr. Hart as being the first medical practitioner in the territory, and Mrs. Coomes as the first school teacher; over twenty of the fortified stations built for protection against the Indians bore distinctive Irish names. Among them Bryan's station, Dougherty's station, Hart's station, Drennan's Lick, Feagan's station, Finn's station, Higgins' block house, Irish station, Lynch's station, McGee station, Sullivan's old station, Sullivan's new station, Sullivan's station, Daniel Sullivan's station, McGuire's station, McCormack's station and McKeenan's station.

Eleven counties in Kentucky bear Irish names: Lyon, Adair, Butler, Logan, Hart, Montgomery, McCracken, Boyle, Carroll, Rowan, Casey. As in New Hampshire and the other colonies, there is not a Gaelic name in Ireland that was not represented in the territory of Kentucky after the Revolution, many of those who bore them being veterans of the War of Independence, a large proportion of whom were living as late as 1840. Their names, published in Collins' history, look like a voting list in South Boston, so unmistakably Irish are they. James McBride, an Irishman, is credited by Collins as being the first white man to enter the territory, "Paddling his canoe up the Kentucky river in

1743." James Mooney, John Finley and William Cool accompanied Daniel Boone to the "dark and bloody ground" in 1769. They were followed in 1775 by Capt. James Grattan, John Toole and John McManus, who laid the foundation of Louisville. Capt. Flynn was one of the founders of Columbia, and with him were John Riley and Francis Dunlevy.

Three of the best known and most daring Indian fighters in Kentucky of the period were Majs. McGarry and McBride and Capt. Bulger, all associates of Daniel Boone. Among the best known Presbyterian clergymen of this early period were Rev. William McGill, Rev. Samuel McAdoo, Rev. Henry Delaney, Rev. A. M. Bryan, Rev. William McGee, Rev. William McMahon and Rev. John Dunlevy. Among the Methodists of the same period were James O'Cool, William Burke, William McMahon and John McGee, all Irish enough in appearance, certainly.

Many of the great names identified with Ireland during the past 200 years are not those peculiar to the province of Ulster, or to the mixed race. Daniel O'Connell, who was the prince of agitators, and who, perhaps, accomplished more during the same period for his people than any man who had preceded him, was from the south of Ireland. Wellington, the iron duke, and the conqueror of Bonaparte, was from Leinster. Moore, the poet, and Balfe, the composer, were from Dublin, in the same province. Plunkett, Grattan, Shiel and the Emmets were all from Munster or Leinster.

Daniel Maclise, the painter, and Sir Charles Barry, the architect of the new house of parliament, were natives of Cork. Goldsmith, of "The Deserted Village," and Parnell, of the Augustan period of English literature, were, like Moore, from Leinster. Arthur Murphy, Edmond and Anthony Malone, Dr. Nugent and Edmund Burke, all contemporaries and intimates of Dr. Johnson, were from Leinster or Munster. Wallace and Sullivan, whose musical productions rank among the best of English-speaking musicians, as well as P. S. Gilmore, the great bandmaster, were from the south of Ireland. Neither Usher, Congreve, Berkeley or Arthur O'Leary had their origin in the north of Ireland.

Search the British records through and the Ulster men who have distinguished themselves either in the army, the navy, or in civil life are by no means in the majority, and this is said without detriment to the many heroic souls the northern Irish province has produced. The Napiers, the O'Haras, the Beresfords, the O'Callaghans, the Nolans, the Kavanaughs, the Butlers, the Burkes of Clanrickhard, the Wolseleys, John Henry Foley, and Dargan, the sculptors, the O'Briens of Inchiquin, the philosophic Boyles, earls of Cork, and thousands who, by conforming to the Established church, had secured places in some one or all of the branches of the government, were none of the Ulster men, and yet our ears are dinned with the constant hum of the superiority of the men from the north of Ireland over those of the other provinces. It is bad enough on the other side of the water, but it is worse here.

Sheridan, one of the most brilliant soldiers thus far produced in America, had no peer among his associates of the army in the Civil War, and Rowan was second to but one in the navy. One was born of Leinster parentage, and the other came here from there. John Roach, the great ship-builder, was from Cork. Charles O'Conor, the great jurist, was the son of a west of Ireland man.

Gen. Meagher was from Waterford. The long line of Kearneys, who furnished eminent representatives to the army and navy for generations, were not of the Ulster stock. Com. John Barry, the father of the American navy,

was from Wexford. The founder of the New Hampshire
Sullivans, one of the most illustrious families of New England, came from Limerick.

Moylan, the dashing commander of the Continental
dragoons, was from Cork. The Carrolls of Maryland, second in eminence to no family in America, were from Leinster. The Burkes of North and South Carolina spring from
Connaught. The Lynches of South Carolina were from the
same province. The Butlers of South Carolina, the Mc-
Henrys of Delaware, the Kavanaghs of Maine, the
O'Reillys, the FitzSimonses, the Shees, the Careys, the
Meades, the Butlers, the Hogans, the Kanes, the Keatings
and the Walshes of Pennsylvania and Kentucky, the O'Fal-
lons of Missouri, the long list of soldiers like Gibbon, Donohoe, Corcoran, Burke, McMahon, Halpine, Riley, Cass,
Guiney, O'Rourke, Smythe, McGinnis, Meade, Gilmore,
Mulligan, Neale and hundreds of others in the Civil War
were not of Ulster.

Grant, from the maternal side, had the blood of the
Kelleys in his veins, and the mother of Farragut was Elizabeth Shine, the daughter of an Irish father. The Ulster
men have had full credit given them for what they have
done for America, but there is enough glory to go round
without robbing the other sections of Ireland of the credit
due for furnishing to the United States some of its greatest
men, of whom the above names are but a few in comparison
to what could be given were it necessary.

SUPPLEMENTARY FACTS AND COMMENT.

REV. DR. REID, in his "History of the Presbyterian Church in Ireland," speaking of the tyranny visited upon the Irish Presbyterians by the British government, writes: "Fines and punishments were inflicted without mercy on the Presbyterians. Many of them had to go to the west of Scotland." This in 1636. Again, he tells us that the Presbyterians were obliged to take the "Black oath," namely, to swear never to oppose any of the king's commands. Those refusing to take it were subjected to the severest treatment. On another page, alluding to the union between the Irish and the Highland Scots in foreign service to support Charles I, in 1644, he writes that the native Irish "from the affinity of language, manners and origin were expected to be well qualified to co-operate with the Highlanders." Again, he tells us that fifteen hundred Irish went to serve in 1645 under Montrose in Scotland. But one of the most significant passages in Reid's work is the statement that in 1610 "All acts forbidding inter-marriages between English, Irish and Scotch were repealed this year to the great joy of all parties." This quite effectually disposes of the fiction, so often put forth by advocates of the " Scotch-Irish " cult, that intermarriages between the different elements in Ulster did not take place. We have conclusive proof here that they did.

THE PLANTATION OF ULSTER.

Mr. Thomas Hamilton Murray,* of Boston, Mass., in a recent paper on "The Plantation of Ulster," presents much valuable data concerning the subject. He expresses amusement over the ridiculous position of the "Scotch-Irish" advocates and the contradictory attitude the latter assume.

"The fact is," he declares, "the cult bases its structure on four propositions—all false and, therefore, worthless. These propositions are: (1) That at the time of the Plantation all of old Irish stock were driven out of Ulster. (2) That the province was repeopled exclusively by Scots. (3) That these were all of Lowland stock. (4) That they never inter-married with other elements in Ireland, but held aloof, wedded only among their kind and thus preserved themselves as 'pure Scots.'

"Now, as a matter of historical truth, none of these conditions obtained. The plantation of Ulster is generally regarded as including the period from 1608 to 1620. At no time before, during or since this period has Ulster been vacated en masse by its Irish population of the older stock. Thousands of this stock, it is true, did emigrate at different times, but other thousands remained and their descendants reside in Ulster to this day.

"At the time of the Plantation, the escheated territory in Ulster, comprising six counties, was practically divided into three parts. The first of these parts was assigned to English undertakers or planters, the second to Scotch and the third to servitors and Irish natives. To the English undertakers were set apart seven precincts or districts; to the Scotch, 9; and to the servitors and Irish natives, 9. Among the Irish natives to whom land was thus set apart at this time in Ulster are found such names as:

O'Neill,	O'Hanlon,
O'Donnell,	O'Gormley,

* Secretary-General, American-Irish Historical Society.

O'Devin,
O'Develin,
O'Hagan,
O'Donnelly,
O'Quin,
O'Corr,
O'Mulholland,
O'Mallen,
O'Boyle,
O'Gallagher,
O'Cassidy,
O'Corcoran,
O'Flanegan,
O'Skanlan,
O'Reilly,
O'Sheridan,
O'Gowan,
O'Bradie,
O'Mulchrewe,
O'Dowgan,
O'Deveney,
O'Seren,
O'Cleary,
O'Muldoon,
MacCann,

MacDonnell,
MacMurphy,
MacNamee,
MacAmallan,
MacGunchenan,
MacSwyne,
MacQuin,
MacCree,
MacArte,
MacGillpatrick,
MacBryan,
MacOwen,
MacHugh,
MacAwley,
MacEnabb,
MacDevett,
MacElynan,
MacCorr,
MacWorrin,
MacGauran,
MacKernan,
MacTully,
MacCormock,
MacShane,
and many others.

"Even were no other proof available, the foregoing list would conclusively show that the people of old Irish stock were not entirely driven out of Ulster, but that a very numerous and important portion remained. Not only did they remain, but they increased and multiplied. Marriages between the English, Scotch and Irish in Ulster also became frequent and in 1610 the law forbidding such marriages was repealed "to the great joy of all parties." Among the native Irish in Ulster to whom land was allowed at the time of the

Plantation, and as part of the Plantation, were the following, the number of acres allowed each being also given:

NAME.	ACRES.
Arte O'Neile (son of the Baron, and half brother of the Earl of Tyrone)	2000
Henry O'Neale (son of Shane)	1500
Tirlagh O'Boyle, gent	2000
Donough McSwyne (Banagh), gent	2000
Hugh McHugh Duffe O'Donnell, gent	1000
Sir Mulmory McSwyne-na-Doe, knight	2000
Bryan Crossagh O'Neale (son of Sir Cormack), gent	1000
Bryan Maguyre, gent	2000
Con McShane O'Neale, gent	1500
Mulmorie McHugh Connalagh O'Rely, gent	2000
Mulmorie Oge O'Reylie, gent	3000
Mulmorie McPhilip O'Reilie, Esq	1000
Hugh O'Reylie, Esq	1000
Con Boy O'Neale	1160
Tirlagh O'Neale, Esq	3330
Walter McLaughlin McSwyne, gent	896
Tirlagh Magwire, gent	500
Bryan McKernan, gent	400
Christopher Nugent, gent	450
Felim McGawran, gent	1000
Shane McHugh O'Reily, gent	475
Shane McPhilip O'Reily, gent	900
Owen McMulmorie O'Reily, gent	500
Gerald Fleming, Esq	475
Walter, Thomas, and Patrick Bradie	800
Bryan O'Coggye O'Reily	400
Morish McTully	300
Bryan O'Neale, gent	1500
Honora Bourk, or Widow O'Boyle	403
Charles O'Neale, gent	360

NAME.	ACRES.
Neal Roe O'Neal	200
Felim and Brian O'Hanlon, gents	200
Carbery McCan, gent	360
Tirlogh Groome O'Hanlon, gent	140
Shane McShane O'Hanlon, gent	100
Shane McOghie O'Hanlon, gent	100
Rorie McFerdoragh O'Hanlon, gent	120
Shane Oge McShane Roe O'Hanlon, gent	120
Loughlin O'Hagan, gent	120
Neale O'Neale, Esq	800
Donough Reogh O'Hagan, gent	100
Donough Oge McMurphie, gent	180
Colla McArte McDonell, gent	120
John and Connor O'Reilly, gents	300
Cahir McOwen (O'Reilly), gent	300
Cahell McOwen O'Reyly, gent	300
Donell McOwen (O'Reyly), gent	150
Owen O'Sheredan (or O'Sheridan), gent	200
Cahill McBrien O'Reily, gent	100
Mulmore McHugh McFarrall O'Reyly, gent	300
Cormacke McGawran	175
Hugh McManus Oge Magauran, gent	150
Breene Oge McGauran, gent	200
Mulmorie McTirlagh O'Reily, gent	200
Felim, Brian, and Cahir O'Reyly	200
Tirlagh McHugh McBryan Bane O'Reylie	150
Donnell McFarrall Oge McKernan, gent	100
Callo O'Gowne (or O'Gowan), gent	150
Shane McCabe, gent	200
Bryan McShane O'Reyly, gent	300
Donill Backagh McShane O'Reyly, gent	200
Wony (or Una) McThomas McKernan, gent	100
Hugh McBrien O'Reyly, gent	100

NAME.	ACRES.
Terence Braddy (or Brady), gent	150
Rorie McPatrick McCan, gent	120
Cormac McTirlagh Brassilagh, gent	120
Neece Quin	120
Hugh McGilleduffe, gent	120
Felim O'Quin	100
Hugh O'Neale	120
Edmond Oge O'Haggan, gent	120
Owen Roe O'Quin, gent	140
Bartholomew Owen, gent	120
Owen O'Corr, gent	120
Brian O'Develin, gent	120
Laghlen O'Hagan, gent	120
Mary Ny Neal (daughter of Sir Cormack)	120
Neale Garrow McRorie O'Donnell, gent	128
Caffer McHugh Duffe O'Donnell, gent	128
Hugh Boy McQuin, gent	128
Donell McQuin, gent	128
Hugh Boy McSwyne (McSweeney), gent	128
Patrick Crone McCree, gent	128
Owen McGillpatrick, gent	128
Grany Ny Donnell	128
Cormack O'Cassida (O'Cassidy), gent	100
Donough Oge Maguire, gent	100
Felim Oge Magwire, gent	190
Redmond Gillpatrick Magwire, gent	190
Shane McHugh, gent	350
Donough Oge McDonaghy Magwire, gent	145
Bryan Oge Magwire, gent	145
Rorie Magwire, gent	100
Tirlogh Moyle Magwire, gent	300
Patrick McDonell, gent	120
Shane McEnabb, gent	130

NAME.	ACRES.
Patrick McHugh Magwire, gent...............	140
Bryan O'Corcoran, gent......................	120
Edmund McBryan McShane, gent..............	140
Felim Duffe McBrien, gent....................	100
Bryan McMulrony (McDonell), gent............	240
John Magwire, gent..........................	140
Donell Groome McArte, gent..................	150
Hugh O'Flanegan, gent......................	192
Cormac Oge McHugh, gent....................	180
Cormock McCollo Magwire, gent..............	144
Connell McWorrin, gent......................	100
Moriertagh O'Flanegan, gent.................	100
Thomas Braddy (Brady)......................	150
Connor McShane Roe O'Bradie, gent...........	150
Henry Betagh (Beatty), gent..................	262
Philip and Shane O'Reily, brothers.............	300
Hugh Roe McShane O'Reily...................	200
Hugh McGlasney (O'Reily), gent..............	100
Barnaby Reily, gent..........................	150
Richard Magwire, gent.......................	120
Shane McDonell Ballagh, and Brian O'Skanlan....	120
Rorie McDonough Magwire, and Patrick Ballagh Magwire, gents.............................	190
Tirlagh Mergagh Magwire, and Felim Duffe McRorie Magwire, gents......................	100
Thomas McJames McDun Magwire Bryan McJames McDun Magwire.. Hugh McJames McDun Magwire..	120
Connor McTirlagh (McDonell), gent............	100
James Sheale (or Shiel).......................	120
Patrick McManus O'Hanlon, and Ardell Moore O'Mulchrewe	120
Brian Oge O'Hagan, gent....................	100

NAME.	ACRES.
Ardill McFelim O'Hanlon, gent	80
Henry O'Neale, gent	60
Donill McShane (surnamed "Mallatus")	60
Hugh McDonnell O'Neale, gent	60
Cormock McNemee, gent	60
Tirlagh Oge McBrian O'Neale, gent	60
Rorie O'Gormley, gent	60
Jenkin O'Devin, gent	60
Henry Oge O'Neale, gent	60
Bryan O'Neale, and Neal Roe	60
Art McRowie O'Neale, gent	60
Hugh Groome O'Hagan, gent	60
Arte McArte O'Neale, gent	60
Felim McAmallan, gent	60
Shane McDonell Groome O'Donnily, gent	60
Shane Roe O'Neale, gent	60
Tirlagh Oge O'Gormeley, gent	60
Hugh McCawell, gent	60
Hugh McHugh Mergagh O'Neale, gent	60
Randal McDonnell, gent	60
Felim Oge O'Mulcreve, gent	60
Fardoragh McBrian Carragh O'Neale, gent	60
Con McTirlagh O'Neale, gent	60
Shane McHugh McAderany O'Donilly, gent	60
Owen O'Hagan, gent	60
Caragh O'Donilly, gent	60
Fardoragh McCahir O'Mallen, gent	60
Shane McLaughlin O'Donnily, gent	60
Teig McEdmond Oge O'Hagan, gent	60
Neale O'Quin, agent	60
Felim Boy O'Haggan, gent	60
Hugh Groome O'Mulchallane (or O'Mulholland), gent	60

NAME.	ACRES.
Fardoragh O'Haggan, gent....................	60
James McGunchenan, gent.....................	60
Manus McNeale McSwyne (McSweeney)..........	64
Farroll McHugh O'Galchor (O'Gallagher), gent...	64
Donnell Groome McArte......................	64
Donell McCormock, gent.....................	50
Coconaght McHugh, gent.....................	50
Donough Oge McHugh, gent..................	50
Felim McAwly, gent...........................	50
Donough McRorie (Magwire), gent..............	50
Shane McDevitt, gent........................	60
Shane Evarr Magwire, gent....................	96
Brian McFelim Roe McDonnell Shane McTirlogh O'Neale.... Hugh McCarbery O'Neale.... }	240
Mulmory McDonell, gent..... Arte McTirlagh O'Neale, gent Neale McTirlagh O'Neale, gent }	240
Eugene Valley (Owen Ballagh) O'Neyle Felim McTirlagh Brasselagh O'Neill... Donnell McHenry O'Neile........... Edmond Oge O'Donnelly............ }	540
Hugh McTirlagh O'Neale. Art McTirlagh O'Neale... Henry McTirlagh O'Neale }	240
Murtagh O'Dowgan........... Owen Modder McSwine....... Owen McMorphy............. Donell O'Deveney.... ...., Donough O'Seren............. Calvagh McBryan Roe McSwine Neal McSwine............. .... }	1000

NAME.	ACRES.
Donnell Ballach O'Galchor (O'Gallagher)	
Dowltagh McDonnell Ballach.........	
Edmond Boy O'Boyle...............	
Tirlagh Oge O'Boyle, Irrel O'Boyle....	
Cahir McMalcavow (O'Boyle)........	960
Shane McTirlagh (O'Boyle)..........	
Dowlatagh McGillduffe, Farrell........	
McTirlagh Oge (O'Boyle), Loy O'Cleary and Shane O'Cleary	
Owen Oge McOwen, and Owen McOwen Edeganny	128
Owen McCoconaght Maguire	
Rorie McAdegany Magwire..	150
Donnell Oge O'Muldoon....	
Donel McCan, gent............................	80
Redmond McFerdoragh O'Hanlon..............	60
Edmond Groome McDonell.....................	80
Alexander Oge McDonell......................	83
Brian, son of Melaghlin, son of Arte O'Neale, gent..	60
Tirlagh Oge McTirlagh Brasselagh, gent..........	60
Hugh McBrian McCan........................	80
Cormock McBryan Magwire, gent..............	96
Meloghlin Oge McCorr, gent..................	50
Hugh Boy Magwire, gent.....................	96
Patrick McHugh, gent........................	50
Garrett and John Magwire, gents..............	60
Donough Magauran, gent......................	75
Richard Fitzsimons...........................	50
Thomas McJames Bane (O'Reily), gent..........	50
Shane Bane O'Moeltully (or Flood), gent........	50

Many others were granted smaller tracts. The law provided that "The above grantees [were] to hold for ever, as of the Castle of Dublin, in common socage, and subject to the Conditions of the Plantation of Ulster."

Continuing, Mr. Murray in his article states that "many of these Irish grantees were of the noblest and most ancient blood in Ireland. In addition to the foregoing and other Irish for whom land was set aside in Ulster, thousands of others remained in the Plantation as laborers and in similar humble capacities. Their presence was essential even to the English and Scottish settlers who needed strong arms to till their vast estates. Nor were the Irish grantees of estates segregated in, or confined to, certain of the counties of the Plantation, as is frequently supposed. On the contrary, they are found in about every county of the Plantation. Thus the 2000 acres set aside to Arte O'Neile were in Armagh, as were the 1500 set aside to Henry McShane O'Neale. The 3330 acres marked off for Tirlagh O'Neale were in Tyrone. The 2000 acres held by Donough McSwyne were in Donegal. Bryan Maguyre's 2000 acres were in Fermanagh. Felim McGawran's 1000 were in Cavan. The 2000 acres assigned Mulmorie McHugh Connalagh O'Rely, and Mulmorie Oge O'Reylie's 3000 were also in Cavan, and so on.

"As for the Irish who were not officially rated as knights or gentlemen, or who were not grantees of large estates, they were probably found in every county, vale and district, even in those that had been granted to the English and Scottish planters. In some of these latter districts they may have equalled, so far as numbers went, the new comers.

"Reid in his 'History of the Presbyterian Church in Ireland' declares that the theory, frequently held, that the Plantation of Ulster dispossessed and displaced the entire native population of Ulster is a decided exaggeration. He also declares that the majority of the Plantation tenents of the British undertakers or colonists were Irish, the original inhabitants of Ulster.

"The idea sometimes entertained by a certain class of

'Scotch-Irish' writers, in the United States, that Ulster of the Plantation was peopled exclusively by Scots is ridiculous and not in accordance with the facts, as this article easily shows. Of the Scots who did settle in Ulster at that period not all of them, by any means, came from the Lowlands. Argyle and other Highland districts furnished many, as writers well informed on the subject have shown. For so many centuries, even before the Plantation, did people migrate from the Scottish Highlands to Ulster, that the amount of Highland blood in the northern Irish province to-day must be far greater than that of Lowland derivation, but so thoroughly mixed and assimilated have become the Scandinavian, English, Scotch, French, Dutch, old Irish and other elements in Ulster, that to attempt to intelligently analyze and classify the exact proportion of each would be a hopeless task.

In a paper on "Certain Scottish Names Derived from Irish Ones," Mr. T. H. Murray, whom we have just quoted, gives us much very interesting data relative to surnames in Ireland and Scotland. In the course of his paper he incidentally presents the following significant list :

O'Neill,	.	.	MacNeill.
O'Duff,	.	.	MacDuff.
O'Kean,	.	.	MacKean.
O'Kenny,	.	.	MacKenny.
O'Lane,	.	.	MacLane.
O'Lean,	.	.	MacLean.
O'Duffie,	.	.	MacDuffie.
O'Kane,	.	.	MacKane.
O'Nichol,	.	.	MacNichol.
O'Donald,	.	.	MacDonald.
O'Donnell,	.	.	MacDonnell.
O'Connell,	.	.	MacConnell.

O'Morrison,	.	.	MacMorrison.
O'Lanahan, .	.	.	MacClannahan.
O'Lennon, .	.	.	MacLennan.
O'Daniel,	.	.	MacDaniel.
O'Murray, .	.	.	MacMurray.
O'Cooney, .	.	.	MacCooney.
O'Cleary, .	.	.	MacCleary.
O'Cawley, .	.	.	MacCawley.
O'Loughlin,	.	.	MacLachlan.
O'Donough,	.	.	MacDonough.

"Many names, mistakingly supposed by some to be peculiar to Scotland—such as Burns, Campbell, Graham, Kerr, Cummin and the like—abound in Ireland, and have so abounded from a remote period. Many of them are of Irish Gaelic origin. The Scotch Nicholsons, for intsance, trace descent from an ancient Irish source. An Irish form of the name was O'Nichola, from which derive MacNichol, MacNicol, Nicholson, Nicolson, etc. A family tradition is that the progenitors of the name in Scotland migrated from Ireland a thousand years ago and settled on the isle of Skye. This tradition is still current in the family and is given full credit.

" Many eminent Scottish families have descended from the Three Collas, Irish lords who flourished in the fourth century of the Christian era. One of these Collas.—Colla Uais,—became monarch of Ireland about A.D. 322—357. Later, he was deposed, and with the two other Collas "and their principal chiefs, to the number of 300," were banished to Scotland (O'Hart's Irish Pedigrees). Eventually, however, the decree of banishment was recalled and they were invited to return to Ireland. O'Hart declares that ' From the Three Collas descended many noble families in Ulster, Connaught, Meath and Scotland.' Among the families of this race—the Clan Colla—were Agnews, Alexanders, Mac-

Allisters, MacArdles, MacDougalds, MacDougalls, Mac-
Dowells, MacVeaghs, MacDonalds and MacDonnells of the
Hebridies, MacOscars, MacGraths, MacTullys, MacCabes,
MacGilmores, MacKennas, MacMahons, MacCanns, Ma-
guires, Boylans, Cassidys, Keenans, Connollys, Magees,
O'Carrolls, O'Flanagans, O'Hanlons and many others of
note.

"An important fact not known to advocates of the
'Scotch-Irish' cult or, if known, seldom or never remembered by them, is this: that of the people who came to
Ulster from Scotland at the time of the Plantation, all were
by no means Scots, 'pure' or otherwise. Especially is this
true of the colonists who were from the Lowlands. The
composite and shifting character of the population of that
part of Scotland at the period mentioned is well known.
Reid in his history of the Irish Presbyterian church says of
the people who settled in Ulster at the period of the Plantation, including those from Scotland, that they were of
different names, nations, dialects, tempers, breeding. This
is a very important point and should be remembered, especially by those who talk so incessantly of their alleged
'pure Scotch' origin. Some of them, we fear, would find it
as difficult to prove that they have any Scotch blood in their
veins as to disprove that they have in their makeup a large
amount of old Irish blood."

ANOTHER SPLENDID EXPRESSION OF FACTS.

A syndicated article published in several leading American papers a few years since, in speaking of the Plantation
of Ulster, says:

"Some tracts were settled entirely with English and
Scotch, others with enterprising Irish, but still more with a
mixture of the two. Each race supplied what the other
lacked. * * * If any one had said in 1692 that a Brit-

ish parliament could succeed in exiling 300,000 Protestant Irish and perhaps an equal number of Catholic Irish in such a way as to make them fight side by side with Catholic Frenchmen and non-sectarian colonists against the United Kingdom, he would have been denounced as a fool. The wise men would have told him that legislative folly might do wonders, but it could not work miracles. Yet that is just what parliament accomplished; for scarcely was the ink dry on the treaty of Limerick (which provided that Catholics should enjoy in Ireland 'such rights as they had enjoyed in the reign of Charles II'), when it was violated by a series of laws that now make honest Englishmen blush. It is needless to repeat the black details. Says one British writer: 'The laws were so many and so atrocious that an Irishman could scarcely draw a full breath without breaking a law.'

"At the same time they [the government] fell upon the Presbyterians of the north, declaring all their marriages illegal and arresting ministers for 'living in adultery'—with their own wives! On top of this came statutes forbidding Catholic or Protestant to manufacture or export to any other country than England. The result was a general flight of the bravest and best—the 'wild geese,' as they were called, from the south to France and Spain (where such names as O'Donoju, O'Donnel and MacMahon still attest their talents and valor), and the men of the north to New England and Pennsylvania, where such local names as Antrim and Derry, Sligo, Tyrone and Belfast show the origin of their families.

"Later there was a combined movement of Celt and Saxon Irishman, Catholic, Quaker and Presbyterian, to South Carolina; and of all colonies sent out by the prolific isle this probably contained the largest proportion of talent, courage and persistent energy. At any rate it may challenge comparison with any other. It is scarcely possible to make a list of the names of the emigrants to South Carolina in 1750-70 without its seeming to be a partial list of America's eminent patriots—Jackson, Calhoun, O'Kelly, McDuffie, Polk, Crockett, Houston, Adair, McKemy, McWhorter, O'Farrell, O'Grady, McNairy. All these are of Irish extraction, and still (some of them Americanized by dropping the O' or Mac) adorn the annals of their states or the nation.

"In 1765 a shipload of emigrants left Carrickfergus for Charleston, and it is claimed that every family in it has since been represented, and some of them many times, in the congress of the United States. On this ship were Andrew Jackson, his wife and two sons, and two years after their location at the Waxhaw settlements, and after the father's death, was born a third son, named for his father, who was destined to humble British pride at New Orleans."

CULLEN'S "STORY OF THE IRISH IN BOSTON."

Cullen's "Story of the Irish in Boston," touching upon the misnomer "Scotch-Irish" and referring to early Protestant Irish in Boston, says: "Perhaps the most significant thing in this connection appears in the organization of the Charitable Irish Society. Without the slightest equivocation they describe themselves as 'of the Irish nation,' and to make the matter plainer, select St. Patrick's day as the time of starting their work. A Scots' Charitable Society had been in existence some sixty years, and was then in a flourishing condition; so if they were Scotchmen, they had no need to call themselves Irishmen, and leave it for modern historians to undo their work."

The Charitable Irish Society of which Cullen speaks was founded on March 17, 1737, by Irish Protestants and is still in existence. Its preamble read as follows:

"Whereas; Several Gentlemen, Merch^{ts} and Others, of the Irish Nation residing in Boston in New England, from an Affectionate and Compassionate concern for their countrymen in these Parts, who may be reduced by Sickness, Shipwrack, Old age and other Infirmities and unforeseen Accidents, Have thought fitt to form themselves into a Charitable Society, for the relief of such of their poor and indigent Countrymen, without any Design of not contributing towards the Provision of the Town Poor in general as usual. And the said Society being now in its Minority, it is to be hoped and expected, that all Gentlemen, Merch^{ts}, and others of the Irish Nation, or Extraction, residing in, or trading to these Parts, who are lovers of Charity and their Countrymen, will readily come into and give their Assistance to so laudable an undertaking; and for the due Regulation and Management of said intended Charity, the Society, on the 17th day of March, in the year 1737, agreed on the following Rules and orders."

Then follow the rules and orders in detail, comprising thirteen sections in addition to the By-Laws. Section VIII declared that "The Managers of this Society shall be a President, a Vice President, a Treasurer, three Assistants, and three Key-keepers, with a Servitor to attend the Society's service, the Managers to be natives of Ireland, or natives of any other Part of the British Dominions of Irish Extraction, being Protestants, and inhabitants of Boston."

The founders of this Society give no indication at any time that they ever heard of the term "Scotch-Irish."

A WORD TO PRESIDENT ELIOT.

W. H. Drummond, M. D., a Protestant Irishman, Montreal, Canada, writing to the Boston Pilot, November, 1896, in condemnation of the term "Scotch-Irish," thus comments:

"President Eliot informs us in an explanatory letter 'that the distinction between the Scotch-Irish and the Irish is very important, the Scotch-Irish being mainly Protestant, and the Irish proper being mainly Catholic.' This, of course, means that Protestants of Irish birth are mainly Scotch-Irish. How much truth is contained in this statement? The province of Ulster included among its population of two to three hundred years ago many people of Scottish birth, and bearing surnames regarded by genealogically illiterate people of today as being distinctively Scotch in origin. But although these immigrants were almost to a man adherents of the Protestant faith, yet Celtic genealogists know perfectly well that in the great majority of cases they were descendants of Irish septs and tribes, who had gone in successive waves of emigration to the Highlands of Scotland.

"Who can doubt the Irish paternity of a race which includes the names of MacNeill (O'Neill), MacRae (McGrath), MacDonald (O'Donnell), MacInnes (McGuinness), MacLennan (McClenaghan), MacKinley (McGinley), MacBrien (O'Brien), etc., etc.? These men might have modified their views on theological matters, but that fact did not effect any change in their Celtic nationality; they were of precisely the same stock and spoke practically the same language as their Catholic brethren in Ireland. Further, in many cases they married native-born Irish wives, as their Norman and Saxon congeners had done before them, revivifying the old nationality and becoming in their sturdy descendants as Irish as the most exacting Hibernian could possibly desire. How does President Eliot define the large number of Englishmen descended from the conquering Norman, and bearing anglicized names? Does he (or any body else) always insist upon their being dubbed French-English? How would President Eliot classify, for instance, our own Canadian statesmen, the Blakes, Baldwins,

Sullivans, O'Briens, Davins, McCarthys? or the Smith O'Briens, and Lord Edward Fitzgeralds of days gone by in Ireland, and these are the names of Protestant Irishmen. Would President Eliot term these men 'Scotch-Irish?'

"It seems to me that if the Harvard gentleman wishes to describe racially the majority of the Protestant settlers of Ulster he will come fairly near the mark by designating them as 'Irish-Scotch-Irish,' but so far as I know, although Irish-Protestants may at times differ with their Catholic fellow-countrymen, yet they are content to be termed 'Irish,' or still better, 'Irish-Irish,' as they have quite enough to answer for without being arraigned before the world as 'Scotch-Irish.' "

FROM A NEW HAMPSHIRE TOWN.

Hon. James F. Brennan, of Peterborough, N. H., one of the State Library Commissioners, in an address at the celebration of the 150th anniversary of Peterborough, Oct. 24, 1889, said: "In what I have to say I shall not refer to the comparatively modern generation of Irishmen—Murphy, Brennan, Hamill, Noone, and scores of others—and their descendants, who have helped to build up this town, and whose history should be left for a resume of fifty years hence, but to those early settlers who came across the ocean, and their descendants; men who risked all, even life itself, to make this spot a fit place for the abode of men. They were composed in a very small part of Scotchmen, Englishmen and other nationalities, but the essential part of the pioneers of our town, in fact nearly all of them, were Irishmen, for I assume that where men were born in Ireland, as they were, where many of their fathers, perhaps, also, some of their grandfathers were born, they were men who can unqualifiedly be called Irishmen.

"Adopt any other standard and a large part of the inhabitants of Ireland at the time they emigrated would not be considered Irishmen, and probably few persons in this town to-day would be considered Americans. The Scotchmen who came to Ireland, and from whom some of the pioneers of this town trace their ancestry, landed on that Emerald Isle, as our town history records it, in 1610, more than a century before their descendants came to this country. They were indeed Irishmen to the manor born, with all the traits, impulses and characteristics of that people, having, as the Rev. Dr. Morison said in his centennial address, the 'comic humor and pathos of the Irish,' and to their severe character and habits 'another comforter came in, of Irish parentage; the long countenance became short, the broad Irish humor began to rise.'

"Thus we see that there are comparatively few persons in town to-day, with the exception of recent comers, who have not coursing in their veins the blood of those sturdy Irishmen who made this town what it is, whose bodies have long since returned to clay in the old cemetery on the hill, and whose history is the history of the town itself. Long may their memory be cherished! Long may the pride which exists in such ancestry be retained! They were brave, honest, manly men, who broke down the barriers that civilization might enter. Their lot was a life of hardship; it is ours to enjoy the fruits of their work.

"Not only the privations of this cold, uninviting country were theirs to suffer, but intolerance and bigotry met them at the threshold of the country to which they were about to bring a blessing. Rev. Dr. Morison in his centennial address, said that when the Smiths, Wilsons, Littles and others arrived, 'it was noised about that a pack of Irishmen had landed.' They were denied even lodgings. Mr. Winship, of Lexington, who extended a welcome to them, however, said, 'If this house reached from here to Charlestown, and I could find such Irish as these, I would have it filled up with Irish, and none but Irish.'

"If there is a town or city in this broad land owing a greater debt of gratitude to that green isle over the sea than does this town, I know it not. If there is a place which should extend more earnest and loving sympathy to Ireland in her struggles, I know not where it is. It was there that your forefathers and mine were born; there where their infant feet were directed; there where they were educated in those grand principles of honesty, sturdy manhood and bravery well fitting them to become the pioneers of any country, and fortunate it was for that land toward which they turned their faces. Here they built their log cabins, and shrines to worship God, and reared families of from eight to sixteen children, for they were people among whom large families were popular, and the more modern aversion to a large number of children had not taken possession of those God-fearing men and women. * * * In reviewing the character of these men, we should not, as a first essential, go into an inquiry of how they worshipped God; or what were their religious or political beliefs; whether Protestant or Catholic, Whig or Tory. We only ask were they honest men, holding fast to those principles which they believed right? The answer to this will not bring the blush of shame upon our cheek, nor the consciousness of regret that their blood is part and parcel of our bodies. If we follow in their footsteps in our dealings with men; if we are as honest and courageous as they; if we do an equal share to make the world better and more attractive to future generations, we can, when the toil of this life is over, rest in the secure belief of duty well done."

A BLOW AT THE "SCOTCH-IRISH" CULT.

Mr. Charles A. Hanna has recently brought out a work on the "Scotch-Irish, or the Scotch in North Britain, North Ireland and North America." The typography of the work is up-to-date, the binding is excellent, but that is about the limit of the value of the production. Fine typography and excellent binding do not make history, though they have been and, we presume, will continue to be, utilized to pervert it.

Consciously or unconsciously, Mr. Hanna deals a severe blow at the "Scotch-Irish" cult, and this is one of the few points outside the printing and binding that entitle the work to any serious attention. Thus declares Mr. Hanna:

"The term Scotch-Irish is peculiarly American. * * * The name was not used by the first of these emigrants, neither was it generally applied to them by the people whom they met here. They usually called themselves Scotch, just as the descendants of their former neighbors in northern Ireland do to-day. * * * The Quakers and Puritans generally spoke of them as the Irish, and during the Revolutionary period we find a large and influential body of these people joined together at Philadelphia in the formation of a patriotic association to which they gave the distinctively Irish title of 'The Society of the Friendly Sons of St. Patrick.'"

Commenting on the above extract from the work, Mr. Martin I. J. Griffin, the Philadelphia editor, says: "So the historian of these people really tells us that there is no such a people as the Scotch-Irish. It is a hard fact to get over that these people whose immigration began in large numbers after, say 1718, did not use the name nor did any one else in speaking of them. I know they are always spoken of as 'Irish' in all arrival returns and such like papers and documents relating to the newcomers. They did not use the term Scotch-Irish, he tells us, but 'called themselves Scotch.' I haven't been among their records, and so cannot question this latter point, but were they not a queer people to allow themselves in all public statements to be called 'Irish' when they counted themselves 'Scotch' and hated to be called 'Irish,' as Mr. Hanna elsewhere tells us? 'They called themselves Scotch,' says Mr. Hanna, yet when they formed a patriotic association they took the 'distinctively Irish title of The Society of the Friendly Sons of St. Patrick.' What a strange people!"

Continuing, Mr. Griffin remarks: "Mr. Hanna says on the first page of his work: 'The appellation 'Scotch-Irish' is not an indication of a mixed Hiberno-Scottish descent. It was first appropriated as a distinctive race name by, and is now generally applied to, the descendants of the early Scotch-Presbyterian emigrants from Ireland.' That word 'appropriated' is well chosen. The term 'Scotch-Irish' was first applied in Pennsylvania as a term of opprobrium or contempt for a low-graded class. I have found it as early as 1757. Mr. Hanna cites examples of its use in that way in 1763. I have found it as late as 1796. The fact really appears to be, as far as this locality (Pennsylvania) is concerned, that when spoken of officially or in respect these people were called 'Irish,' but when one needed to speak in contemptuous terms he said of such as he desired to apply it to, that they were 'Scotch-Irish'—that is, a low class. So General Lee applied it in 1776, and so I find it in 1757 when an alleged Popish plot was reported to England as existing in Pennsylvania. Little credence was given the information, and in attempting to discover who gave it, it was suspected that it was some one of no account —some 'Scotch-Irishman.' So that's how the term originated in this locality."

Again Mr. Griffin observes: "Some of these people later, and I suspect when the Irish—the Catholic—emigration became great, say from 1830—sought to distinguish themselves from the Catholic Irish, simply 'appropriated' the term 'Scotch-Irish.' They have kept it and by their race pride and persistence in claiming, as well as in fact, have fixed the term to simply mean Protestant Irish. The Catholics are the 'Irish,' just the name the others took when they formed an association. They were once willing, Mr. Hanna shows, to proclaim themselves IRISH. But what a deplorable revelation it is to all of us real Irish who have been boasting about the Friendly Sons of St. Patrick of Philadelphia * * * when Mr. Hanna takes the roll and allows but seven of the members, 'all brave and active patriots,' he concedes, to be Irish, with probably five others who may have been. All the others he counts as his beloved 'Scotch-Irish.' Weren't they very generous to call the society 'Irish' when not over a dozen were really so? If they called themselves 'Scotch,' as Mr. Hanna assures us, why didn't they join the Thistle Society, then existing many years, composed of Scotchmen who were publicly known as Scotch, and proud of the name, too? Irish was a name of credit. So was Scotch. But to call a man a 'Scotch-Irish-man' was really to brand him as of low character. The Scotch were not, in the Revolutionary period, held in high estimation. The original draft of the Declaration of Independence spoke of the 'Scotch mercenaries' coming as an army. This was stricken out in deference to Dr. Witherspoon."

Mr. Hanna's bald assertion that the people now dubbed "Scotch-Irish" usually called themselves "Scotch" is the sheerest nonsense. His assertion that the same element in Ireland to-day calls itself "Scotch" is still more nonsensical, if that were possible, than the other. Mr. Hanna should have greater regard for the intelligence of his readers. Thousands of the descendants of Irish Presbyterians who came here in Colonial days do not now, and never have, referred to themselves as either "Scotch" or "Scotch-Irish." They would very quickly repudiate both terms if applied to them. The few noisy individuals who continually ring the changes on the "Scotch-Irish," and who sing the glory of the latter will hardly relish Mr. Hanna's declaration that "the term Scotch-Irish is peculiarly American. * * * The name was not used by the first of these emigrants, neither was it generally applied to them by the people whom they met here." What Mr. Hanna has done, probably without intending it, is to knock the props from under the whole fabric.

INVENTION OF AN ETHNICAL ABSURDITY.

Mr. Joseph Smith,* of Lowell, Mass., who is also quoted elsewhere in this work, in discussing that ethnical absurdity, the "Scotch-Irice race," observes:

"* * * Worse still, they claimed everything for a race which they themselves had created, and which they christened with the ridiculous title of Scotch-Irish. The average Scotchman and Irishman seemed to be in the dark about it: what it was or where it came from puzzled ethnologists; we had to be content with the information that it was a miracle-working, marvellous people, having all human virtues and many heavenly halos, and that it was discovered simultaneously somewhere in New Hampshire or Pennsylvania, and in a similarly definite locality in Tennessee. * * * The only reasonable and plausible cause (for the term) must be looked for in pure, bald religious arrogance and intolerance, and a wish to separate the Irish race into two clans on religious grounds,—the Catholic or 'Irish-Irish,' and the Protestant or 'Scotch-Irish.'

"This looks like the attribution of mean motives to men, but no other explanation presents itself. And if this sort of logic is good there is no reason why the Turks should not be called Moors, for both profess Moslemism;

---

* Author of The "Scotch-Irish" Shibboleth Analyzed and Rejected.

or why the French, Spaniards, and Italians should not be called Irishmen, since all are in religion Catholics. Such primary school logic is good as far as it goes ; but it doesn't go far, even in Pennsylvania, Tennessee, or Canobie Lake.

"A certain other class of writers has been exploiting the 'Anglo-Saxon' race, ascribing to it virtues and attributes almost divine. But as Anglo-Saxonism has in the end proved to be merely John Bullism, sensible people have turned the mythical animal over to after-dinner speakers and emotional parsons. The passing of the Anglo-Saxon, however, has left an aching void in the hearts and emotions of certain people who wanted a 'race' of their own to brag about. They wouldn't have the Anglo-Saxon at any price ; they were not Germans or French or Italians or Spanish ; they fought shy of the Scotch ; they shrieked at the Irish, and they apparently did not understand that the term American was good enough for anybody. In this hysterical crisis they invented that ethnical absurdity, the Scotch-Irishman, and Scotch-Irish race. Just what the Scotch-Irish race is, who the Scotch-Irish are, where they come from, what they look like, where their habitat is, are questions that no fellow seems able to answer.

"Perhaps the man who comes nearest to supplying this aching void, and telling us who and what this marvellous, ethnic paragon is, is the Rev. John S. MacIntosh, of Philadelphia, in his highly entertaining monograph styled, 'The Making of the Ulsterman.' Let us in a grave and reverent spirit examine this gentleman's masterpiece of imaginative literature.

"He opens his wonderful story with a meeting in Antrim, Ireland, of three men—a Lowlander (Scotch), an Ulsterman (Irish), and himself (an American), whom he calls a Scotch-Irishman, though born on the banks of the Schuylkill. He remarks feelingly, after presenting them to the

reader: 'There we were, a very evolution in history.'
They were, in fact, the three Scotch-Irish musketeers; and
there they sat, looking out over the Irish waters toward
the hungry Lowlands of Scotland, pitying the world,
scratching their heads thoughtfully, only remembering how
they had made the United States, without letting anybody
find it out. They talked, figured each other out, and said,
like the big, brawny, red-legged Highlanders they were not:
'Are we not the splendid men entirely?'

"Dr. MacIntosh now proceeds to mix his three musketeers in order to pull the Simon-pure Scotch-Irishman out
of the shuffle. Let us follow him slowly, without mirth, if
possible.

"The first element in the Scotch-Irishman is the Lowland Scotchman. Be sure and get the real article; nothing
else will do. Has it ever occurred to you what a remarkable man the Lowlander is? Probably not. You have
had your eye on the Highlander as the finest fruit of Scotland; but that is all romance and Walter Scott. The Lowlander is the man; whether he be a hollow-chested Paisley
weaver, a penny-scraping Glasgow huckster, or a black-
browed Border cattle-thief.

"Now, who was the Lowlander of MacIntosh? He
was a mixture of Scot, Pict, Norseman, Saxon, Friesian,
Briton, Erse, Norman, and possibly a score of other things.
The same mixture in dogs produces the noble breed we call
a mongrel.

"Motley, in his 'Rise of the Dutch Republic,' * * *
says in effect that the religious wars of Protestant and
Catholic, and the persecutions growing out of them of the
ever-increasing sectaries, drove shoals of artisans from Germany, Holland, and France to England. Elizabeth of
England had troubles of her own, and while she quarrelled
with the Pope and disputed his headship, she was jealously

insistent of her own leadership of her State Church, and had no use for the pugnacious sectaries from across the Channel. In time, owing to the English jealousy of foreigners and rival manufacturers, and the Queen's abhorrence of rivals against divinely-selected kings, Elizabeth shut down on the refugees and refused them asylum. Scotland, then in the throes of religious squabbles, * * * gave them a welcome as kindred spirits. When other days came, when Mary's head had rolled from the block at Fotheringay, when her wretched son was enthroned, the foreign element found Scotland a poor land to live in. The settlement of Ulster gave them their chance, and they flocked there with Scotchmen and Englishmen to settle down and intermarry and become, as all before them had become, in that Irish crucible, Irish."

RELIGION NO TEST OF RACE.

James Jeffrey Roche, LL. D., editor of the Boston Pilot, replying to an article by Henry Cabot Lodge, says in the Pilot, July 9, 1892, "Of course, if we accept Mr. Lodge's definition, that an Irishman of the Protestant religion is not an Irishman, but a Scotchman, more particularly if he be an Englishman by descent, Mr. Lodge's case is proven, even though his own witnesses otherwise contradict him; and equally, of course, a Catholic Irishman becomes a Scotchman, or vice versa, by simply changing his religion.

"In his anxiety to make a point against Catholics by extolling the French Huguenots and 'Scotch-Irish,' Mr. Lodge forgets common sense, and what is worse, forgets common honesty. When he comes to claim especial glory for his own section of the country, he gives away his whole case by saying: 'The criticism that birthplace should not be the test for the classification by communities seems hardly to require an answer, for a moment's reflection ought to convince any one that no other is practicable,' although he hastens to add that 'place of birth is no test of race.'

"Nothing is, apparently, except religion; and the test of that is, whether or not it is Mr. Lodge's own brand of religion. We have not a word to say against the latter, even though in his case, unfortunately, it has not developed an 'ability' for counting correctly or quoting honestly. * * * Irishmen, at least, do not qualify their admiration of national heroes by inquiries into their religion. Protestant Emmet is still the idol of the Irish Catholic; and we doubt if any intelligent Huguenot would give up his share in the glory of Catholic Lafayette."

UNITING WITH THEIR CATHOLIC COUNTRYMEN.

Robert Ellis Thompson, Ph. D., formerly a Professor in the University of Pennsylvania and now President of the Central High School, Philadelphia, speaking of the early Irish Presbyterian immigration to this country, says:

"* * * And these immigrants brought to America such resentments of the wrongs and hardships they had endured in Ireland as made them the most hostile of all classes in America toward the continuance of British rule in this new world, and the foremost in the war to overthrow it. And those who remained in Ulster were not much better affected toward the system of rule they continued to endure. At the close of the century we find the greater part of them uniting with their Roman Catholic countrymen for the overthrow of the monarchy and the establishment of an Irish republic, with the help of the French."

ALL IRISH RECEIVED INTO BROTHERHOOD.

Mr. Thomas Hamilton Murray, of Boston, Mass., writing on this subject to Mr. Eben Putnam, of Salem, Mass., declares:

"It has always been a matter of astonishment to me that persons who ring the changes on the 'Scotch-Irish' display such a superficial knowledge of the plantation of Ulster and of the composition of the people of that province. One would think that before holding forth as exponents of the doctrine, they would first solidly inform themselves as to the conditions of the period and place in question. * * * We of the old Irish race draw no invidious distinctions, but receive into brotherhood all born on Irish soil or of Irish parents, regardless of creed and no matter where their grandfather or great-grandfather may have come from. * * *

"Why anybody of Irish birth or descent should try to sink his glorious heritage and seek to establish himself as 'Scotch rather than Irish,' or rather why anybody should try to do it for him, is something difficult to understand. Ireland possesses a more ancient civilization than either Scotland or England. Her hagiology, her educational institutions, her old nobility, her code of laws, her jurisprudence, are of much greater antiquity. 'The Irish,' declares Collins, 'colonized Scotland, gave to it a name, a literature and a language, gave it a hundred kings, and gave it Christianity.' For additional evidence on this point, see Knight, Lingard, Chambers, Lecky, Venerable, Bede, Buckle, Pinkerton, Logan, Thebaud, Sir Henry Maine, Freeman, the Century Dictionary of Names and other authorities.

"Any writer who honestly aims to give any section of Irish settlers in this country a deserved meed of praise shall always have my respect and encouragement. It is only when Irish are claimed as of Scotch descent who are not, or when exclusive merit is claimed for those who are, I object. It is a fact that thousands of north of Ireland Catholics are of Scottish descent on one side or the other. It is also true that many of the best friends of Irish nationality, autonomy and independence have been of the same element, Protestant and Catholic. But they were simply 'Irish,' look you. They weighted down their birthright with no extenuating prefix or palliating affix. It is a blunder to suppose that all the Irish settlers in New Hampshire were of 'Scottish descent.' Many of the most prominent who located there were not. Yet because some were, hasty writers have jumped to the conclusion that all were of Scotch ancestry. A more lamentable error it would be difficult to fall into.

"In 1766 St. Patrick's Lodge of Masons was instituted at Johnstown, N. Y., being the first lodge organized in that Province west of the Hudson river. The first master of the lodge was an Irishman, Sir William Johnson, a native of the County Meath. On St. Patrick's Day, 1780, a St. Patrick's Lodge of Masons was instituted for Portsmouth, N. H. Later we find Stark's rangers requesting an extra supply of grog so as to properly observe the anniversary of St. Patrick. Very little comfort here for your 'Scotch-Irish' theorist.

"The Massachusetts colonial records repeatedly mention the 'Irish,' not the Scotch-Irish. Cotton Mather in a sermon in 1700 says: 'At length it was proposed that a colony of Irish might be sent over to check the growth of this countrey.' No prefix there. The party of immigrants remaining at Falmouth, Me., over winter and which later settled at Londonderry, N. H., were alluded to in the records of the general court as 'poor Irish.' Marmion's 'Maritime Ports of Ireland' states that 'Irish families' settled Londonderry, N. H. Spencer declares that 'the manufacture of linen was considerably increased by the coming of Irish immigrants.' In 1723, says Condon, 'a colony of Irish settled in Maine.' Moore, in his sketch of Concord, N. H., pays tribute to the 'Irish settlers' in that section of New England. McGee speaks of 'the Irish settlement of Belfast,' Me. The same author likewise declares that 'Irish families also settled early at Palmer and Worcester, Mass.' Cullen describes the arrival at Boston in 1717 of Capt. Robert Temple, 'with a number of Irish Protestants.' Capt. Temple was, in 1740, elected to the Charitable Irish Society. In another place Cullen alludes to 'the Irish spinners and weavers who landed in Boston in the earlier part of the 18th century.'

"The Boston Charitable Irish Society was instituted on St. Patrick's Day, 1737. The founders were all Protestants and described themselves as 'of the Irish nation.' Rev. John Moorhead, a Presbyterian minister of Boston, was born in the north of Ireland and received much of his education in Scotland. Yet he wished to be regarded as mere 'Irish.' In proof of this he joined the society in 1739, and made an address on that occasion. Only men of Irish birth or extraction could be admitted to active membership in the society then as now. Mr. Moorhead in being thus admitted so acknowledged himself. His congregation is described by Drake, Condon, Cullen and other authorities, as being composed of 'Irish-Presbyterians.' There is no mention whatever of any 'Scotch-Irish' in the neighborhood. The founders of this Charitable Irish Society bore such names as Allen, Alderchurch, Boyd, Bennett, Clark, Duncan, Drummond, Egart, Freeland, Gibbs, Glen, Knox, Little, Mayes, McFfall, Moore, Mortimer, Neal, Noble, Pelham, Stewart, St. Lawrence, Thomas, Walker and Walsh—all 'of the Irish nation.'

"Before 1765 the Society also had on its rolls the names: Austin, Arthur, Anderson, Black, Boulton, Ball, Caldwell, Coppinger, Calderwood, Campbell, Draper, Dunning, Dunworth, Derby, Edgar, Elliot, Ellison, Ferguson, Hall, Hutchinson, Holmes, Hill, Hamilton, Lewis, Lee, Motley, Malcolm, Miller, Morton, Nelson, Richey, Richardson, Savage, Stanley, Tabb, Temple, Thompson, Vincent, Williams, Wood, and many others. The bearers of the names mentioned in this paragraph were all, or nearly all, Irish Protestants, yet in no instance whatever do the records of the society refer to any of them as 'Scotch-Irish.' Among the 'Macs' belonging to the society previous to 1770 are found: McCrillis, McClure, McCordey, McCleary, McCarroll, McClennehan, McDaniel, McFaden, McGowing, McHord, McIntire, McIntyre, McLane, McNeil, McNeill, and a number of others—all, as we have before remarked, 'of the Irish nation.'

"The Friendly Sons of St. Patrick, Philadelphia, Pa., organized in 1771, was composed of 'Catholics, Presbyterians, Quakers and Episcopalians,' who were 'united like a band of brothers.' They were never known as 'Scotch-Irish.' The founder of the Friendly Sons of St. Patrick, New York city, was Daniel McCormick, an Irish Presbyterian. The society was instituted in 1784, comprised Catholics, Presbyterians and members of other creeds, and bore on its rolls previous to 1795 such names as Bradford, Barnewell, Constable, Colles, Clinton, Charleton, Edgar, Gaine, Glover, Gibson, Hill, Lynch, Macomb, McVicar, Pollock, Price, Shaw, Stewart, Templeton, Thomson, Wade and a great many others. From 1804 to 1815 we find on the rolls of the society the following names among others: Wallace, Parks, Searight, Reid, Blake, Rutledge, Cranston, McEvers, Watson, Kemp, Jephson, Chambers, Keith, Bailey, Sterling, Emmet, Macneven, etc. Neither the society nor its members are ever referred to as 'Scotch-Irish.'

"Many persons who continually sing the praises of the so-called 'Scotch-Irish' stand in serious danger of being considered not only ignorant but positively dishonest. Their practice is to select any or all Irishmen who have attained eminence in American public life, lump them together and label the lump 'Scotch-Irish.' * * *

"Prejudiced or poorly informed writers have made sad work of this Scotch-Irish business. Thus Henry Cabot Lodge gives the absurd definition of 'Scotch-Irish' as being 'Protestant in religion and chiefly Scotch and English in blood.' This has only been equalled in absurdity by Dr. MacIntosh, who has defined this elusive element as 'not Scotch nor Irish, but rather British.' Here we have two gentlemen claiming to speak as with authority, yet unable to agree even in first essentials.

"Most people who use the mistaken term 'Scotch-Irish' appear to do so under the supposition that it is synonymous with Protestant-Irish. Not so. Thousands of Protestant Irish are of English descent, with not a drop of Scotch blood in their veins. Other thousands are of Huguenot extraction, a point with which some do not appear to be acquainted. Welsh, Scandinavian, German and Dutch blood also enter materially into this Protestant Irish element.

"Another blunder is made in regarding all Ulstermen as of Scotch descent. With poorly-informed writers the fact that a man hails from the northern province is sufficient to stamp him as 'Scotch-Irish.' To any student of Irish history the fallacy of this is at once evident. Why, some of the most ancient blood in Ireland comes from Ulster, and at the time of the English conquest thousands of Catholic Ulstermen were exiled and scattered far and wide.

"While kittens born in an oven may not be biscuit, it is certain that men born in a country are natives of that country. The Irish Presbyterians were treated with great harshness by various successive governments in England. At one time edicts of banishment were issued against their ministers ; at another we find the government wickedly declaring their pulpits vacant and filling them with clergymen of the Established church. When England had a policy of church or state to carry out in Ireland it could be made to bear as heavily on the Presbyterian as on the Catholic. England's repeated suppression of Irish industries also caused great numbers of Presbyterians and Irish Protestants, generally, to emigrate to America.

"Some of the 'Scotch-Irish' devotees would have us understand that emigration from Scotland to Ireland commenced at the beginning of the 17th century. In this they are over a thousand years out of the way. Migration and emigration between the two countries began many centuries earlier than the 17th, or when Scotland became an Irish colony. When that was can easily be ascertained by giving the matter proper attention and careful inquiry."

During a correspondence, a few years ago, between Mr. Murray and Mr. Samuel Swett Green, of Worcester, Mass., Mr. Green thus manfully wrote:

"In regard to the use of the term Scotch-Irish, I did not realize that I should give offense by employing it, and I probably should have used some other designation to convey my meaning rather than irritate bodies of men whom I respect. I used the word, however, only in a descriptive sense, just as I sometimes use the terms Afro-American and Swedish-American. I entirely agree with Mr. Murray that, generally speaking, it is best not to use words which show the differences of the inhabitants of a country rather than the things which they hold in common. For example, it is better to speak generally of Americans, rather than Irish-Americans or French-Americans."

CATHOLIC AND PROTESTANT HONOR ST. PATRICK.

Hon. John D. Crimmins, of New York city, in his recent work on "Early Celebrations of St. Patrick's Day" (New York, 1902), observes:

"If Ireland in 1737 was economically, nationally and politically dead, Irishmen were in the front of the struggle of life outside her boundaries. Swordplay there was in plenty on the continent of Europe. The wars of the Polish and Austrian successions involved most of the continental powers, and there were Irishmen in every battle. Nothing was heard then in Ireland, England, Europe or America of the distinction made by ill-instructed moderns between the Irish and the 'Scotch-Irish,' the latter a racial figment adopted since by shallow commentators of no ethnological standing. * * *

"Our Protestant Irishmen at Boston who were gayly celebrating the day of the Saint as the Catholic Irish soldiers in the armies of France and Spain were celebrating it in their camps, were simply demonstrating the mental resiliency of the Gael. He cannot remain crushed while life is in him.* * * His ability to find something to smile at while suffering acutely is as characteristic of him to-day as it was two hundred years ago. * * * This saving humor survived the drastic days of Cromwell and stood a friend during the grim, hopeless century between the battle of the Boyne and the battle of Vinegar Hill. The Irish nature was like the Irish climate, its smiles making up for its tears. In such a nature there is no despair. Defeat that leaves it life, is a downfall, not a hopeless calamity.

"Often it has been said that with more consistent grimness of character the Irish would have achieved their aspirations; equally it may be said that with more grimness in them they would have been annihilated. Time and again through great crises of their history they struggled manfully up to a certain point; beyond that they submitted to their fate, however dreary, with a smiling philosophy that was the puzzle of their conquerors. 'They are downtrodden, but surely they are contented, for they dance in the moonlight and sing by the cradle, and laugh and are merry at weddings and christenings,' said the rulers. But they were not contented. Their imaginations clung to the memory of the olden times, and they were ever ready for another effort when events seemed to favor it. Their natures underwent no change. Their songs and laughter were no 'organized hypocrisy,' but simply the vent of ebullient, uncrushable souls."

ARCHBISHOP PLUNKETT OF DUBLIN, IRELAND.

Some years since, the Protestant Archbishop Plunkett of Dublin, Ireland, in receiving a number of visitors, said: "I hope that while we shall always be very proud of our imperial nationality, proud of our connection with the British empire, on the history of which, as Irishmen, we have shed some luster in the past, and from our connection with which we have derived much advantage in return,—while we are proud, I say, of our imperial nationality, let us never be forgetful of our Irish nationality. We may be descended from different races—the Danes, Celts, Saxons, and Scots—but we form a combined stratum of our own, and that is Irish, and nothing else."

FROM ULSTER TO AMERICA.

In his production (1898) on "The 'Scotch-Irish' Shibboleth Analyzed and Rejected," Mr. Joseph Smith, of Lowell, Mass., already quoted, says:

"It is certainly true that a large emigration flowed out of Ulster into America during the eighteenth century, even after the Revolution; but the people who so emigrated were Irish,—plain, strong-limbed, angry, English-hating Irish, who came over the stormy Atlantic with a thorough detestation of England and a hearty contempt of Scotland, and all the tyranny, robbery, oppression, and civil, religious, and political proscription Great Britain represented.

"They and their fathers had lived in Ireland and loved Ireland; and if the habits, customs, loves, hates, ideas, and thoughts gained in an Irish atmosphere, on Irish soil, make Irishmen, these people were Irish. They called themselves Irish; the English on American soil called them Irish and banned them as Irish; they named their settlements after Irish towns; they founded societies which they called Irish; they celebrated St. Patrick's Day in true Irish fashion, and seemed to have no fear that a day would come when a ridiculous association would call them and their children by any other title. Stranger yet, the men who remained behind in Ulster have yet to learn the startling information that they are 'Scotch-Irish.' * * *

"The fact cannot be gainsaid that the Irish-Presbyterians, almost to a man, were against England; but it was their nationality—Irish—and the sufferings entailed on them in Ulster, and not their Presbyterianism, that made them ardent rebels. If further proof were necessary, attention might be called to the fact that all the Scotch settlements in America were ultra-loyal to the British Crown, whether in what is now the United States or in British America. * * *

"Let us mete out justice, fair play, and honorable treatment to the men of all nations, who have helped to make this greatest of the nations, and let us fearlessly and persistently demand them for ourselves. * * *

"It will pay Professor Fiske to examine into the Irish emigration of the eighteenth century and learn, as less erudite people have done, that as much of this stream flowed from Limerick, Cork, Waterford, Dublin, and English Bristol, as from Ulster; and that Leinster and Munster poured in fully as many Irish to Colonial America as did the northern province. What he is unwittingly doing is setting up the abhorrent dividing lines of religion and marking off the race into 'Irish-Irish' and 'Scotch-Irish' upon the lines of Catholicity and Protestantism. I, as one of the Protestant Irish, most strenuously object; the name Irish was good enough for my fathers; their son is proud to wear it as they did; and we must all insist that the Irish, without any qualifications, all children of a common and well-loved motherland, shall be given their full measure of credit for the splendid work done by them in America."

A CONCLUSIVE VIEW OF THE CASE.

Mr. Henry Stoddard Ruggles, Wakefield, Mass., who is an American of the ninth generation, heartily condemns the cant term "Scotch-Irish." Writing on this subject recently, he remarks:

"A man is the sum of his ancestors—not in the male line only, but through all the many female sources as well. The place of a man's birth, unless the law is invoked to amend the matter, fixes his nationality. All are of mixed stocks if pedigree is traced far enough back, and all of us descend both from kings and knaves. The more remote the ancestor in the number of generations, the more dilute is that especial strain, and the fad of searching for some ennobled progenitor in the distant centuries can give one only that which he shares in common with all the world.

"To select a race, inhabiting a contracted section of an island of Europe two centuries ago, imbuing them with the sum of all virtues, placing them, in the characteristics that mark the powers of leadership and success, above all the world, and giving to them power to transmit their gifts and attributes to descendants of the third and fourth generation—yes, and the fifth and sixth—unimpaired by intermarriage with other tribes; and then to enroll oneself among the favored descendants, constitutes a wonderful bit of egotism that the rest of the world may be pardoned for finding a source of amusement. The vanity is harmless enough, certainly, but when this folly goes so far as to give an artificial race distinction to this people not in accord with its origin or the recognized and universal rule of classification, and brand all descendants, willingly or unwillingly, as of this fantastic race, some of these are likely to protest.

"I trace through the male line of my mother to Hugh Ross, of Belfast, Ireland, a Presbyterian Irishman, who emigrated near the beginning of the eighteenth century, settled in Portsmouth, New Hampshire, and later just across the river, in Kittery. I am not prepared to say that his male ancestry did not run into the Highlands of Scotland, for I do not know fully as to his lineage, but through the many other lines it is unquestionable that his derivation was from different stock, probably Irish, for generations. Even if in some earlier ancestor it shall be found that a Ross was of the Highland clan of the far north, it will be necessary only to go farther still to find the forebears of that clan again in Ireland.

"My reading has convinced me that a so-called 'Scotch-Irishman' means simply a Protestant Irishman, whether from Ulster or Munster, but the preference is usually with the man from Ulster. He is the Simon pure article! By this peculiar logic, you see, I derive from the very choicest strain in all creation. I am very proud of my ancestry, but my pride in my Ross origin is that for a good old Irish family, and as I have in my veins, through other lines, blood derived from Scotch sources, of which I justly boast, race prejudice can have nothing to do with my abhorrence for a name false alike to two splendid peoples."

JUDGE WAUHOPE LYNN'S COMMENT.

Judge Wauhope Lynn, New York City, who is of North of Ireland Presbyterian stock, writes as follows, under date of June 19, 1902:

"My Dear Sir:—Your kind letter to hand requesting some expression from me touching the subject of the misnomer called 'Scotch-Irish.' I presume you feel that I could better speak on this matter than some of my countrymen whose ancestry there is less doubt about. We of the County of Antrim, largely made up of Protestants, are presumed to have had our origin from something other than Irish, a statement often made but never proven.

"It would be a hard problem, indeed, to attempt to analyze the exact derivation of any particular class in Ireland, as she has been the home and refuge, in early times, of representatives of all the great peoples of the world. The recent work of Mr. Charles Johnston attempts to give an outline of Irish history, and he finds great mystery in the origin of our people. Certain it is that we have no common affinity, either in temperament or physique, with what is known as the Saxon line, and while many Saxons have found their way into Ireland, their assimilation with the Irish has been so complete that little or no trace of them is left, after a few generations.

"The dominant blood in Ireland is that of the Celt, and while they may have a common affinity with their brothers in Wales, and those in the Highlands of Scotland, there is certainly little with what is known as the Lowland Scot or Saxon Scot. It is true that considerable Scotch came into the County of Antrim during the wars of O'Neill against Queen Elizabeth, but these Scotch were Highland Scotch, like the MacDonalds, who came over from their native Highlands to assist O'Neill in his wars against England.

"Many of this type of people remained in Antrim, and

married with the Irish Celt, and are to-day a prominent feature in the country. The phrase, 'Scotch-Irish,' is a pure invention, and I suspect sometimes it has an anti-Catholic meaning, for I find that only those use it who have in mind a latent opposition to the Catholic Irish. Certain it is that this phrase is not heard of in Ireland, and is more an American invention by that type living here, who are somewhat ashamed to have their ancestry charged with being Irish and prefer to cloak it under the more pleasing title, to them, of 'Scotch-Irish.'

"These men would reason that because many men of the Protestant religion, born in Ireland, have become eminent in various walks of life, that they must have been of different extraction than those of their Catholic brothers. They overlook the important fact that just as many Catholic Irish have reached as high a plane as their Protestant countrymen. This narrow view, however, has been the dominant one, persistently carried out by England in all her governmental affairs in Ireland, that is, to give preference and prominence, as well as emoluments, to Protestant Irish over those of the Catholic faith.

"I resent most strongly the use of the term 'Scotch-Irish,' a term which is not only nonsensical, but which is generally used with a malicious purpose, as it aims to detract from a noble, generous people honor and credit, and give to Scotland merit which she herself never earned, and which her own people never claimed credit for. The Presbyterians of the North of Ireland, of whom form an humble part, have at all times proclaimed themselves to be Irish people, and in the great struggles, by their ministers, men of learning, scholars and lovers of their country, have never refrained from doing and declaring that their hearts and sympathies were with, and a part of, the Irish people.

"The United Irishmen, formed during the rising of

1798, were largely made up of patriotic Presbyterians, and those men at no time in their history were ever characterized or described or admitted they were any other than a part of the great people they were struggling for. The pretence that the Ulster Plantation was made up exclusively of Scotch from the Lowlands is an error. A large part of the Ulster Planters, installed there under King James, were English people, coming from in and around the city of London. The name, Londonderry, is the best evidence of this fact.

"If the Saxon Scots had come in any great numbers to make up the Plantation, certain it would be we would find some evidence in names or nomenclatures. Whatever Scotch came at this particular time were chiefly of the Gael, and the best blood in the North of Ireland to-day, in the particular section from which I came, is the blending of the two great Gaelic families, those of the Highlands of Scotland and those of the North of Ireland. The difficulty heretofore with our students of Irish history has been the confusing with our national types of low-bred types which, in some sections, found their way among our people, but whose presence at no time ever was national. But these types have been the types from which criticism of Irish life has been formed, and on which so much has been said derogatory to our great national life.

"We of the North owe nothing to Scotland, either in high standards, civilization, culture or religion, but, on the contrary, we have given Scotland some of her best blood, some of her purest patriots, some of the brightest pages of her history. England's policy has ever been to mar the patriotic strivings of our race, and, whatever her tools, she has ever striven to blot out that bright spark of our race which has never submitted to her control.

"The best writers are now agreed that not only Scotland, but many parts of England were populated by the scholarly Irish in the early centuries, but her scholars who wandered from their own shores to give learning and intelligence to their brothers in the establishment and founding of colleges and schools are now almost forgotten. British influences are now, as they have long been, endeavoring to rob the Irish people of that rich heritage which God endowed the latter with, the inheritance of character and honor. They have taken our lands by confiscation; they have abolished the Brehon law, which was equal, if not superior, to the law of Justinian; they have given us penal laws and coercion enactments; they had almost destroyed our ancient language. Many of the valuable records preserved in our country they have annihilated. They have drained from our families some of their best sons, and made proselyites of them, to serve as soldiers in foreign wars. They will credit us with nothing, whether it is a Wellington or Wolseley, who gave them half an empire in India; a Roberts, who won for them the only victory in the Boer war; or a Kitchener, who concluded for them a peace which saved them from dishonor. They have taken our poets, and called them British; our orators, and called them English. They have taken our sculptors, and induced them to change their names. They have taken the greatest scientist of the age, Tyndall, and absorbed him in their British category.

"But, after all, why should we be angry at the shortcomings of those who wish and prefer to misunderstand or misrepresent us. If they were fair critics we might hope to enlighten them. If they were just judges we might bring evidence before them to convince them of their error; if they were kindly disposed towards our people we might point out to their better judgment the true conditions.

"The critics of the Irish are not found in France, where

the Irish have always had a welcome and a generous reception; the critics of Ireland are not found in Germany, where her best college has established a chair for the teaching of the Irish language; they are not found in Italy, where monuments are found dedicated to Irish worthies; they are not found in Russia, for some of Ireland's best sons have given strength to that mighty empire; they are not found in Spain, for which the Irish won so many honors; they are not found in Scotland or in Wales, where the common ties of race make the Irish people respected. The critics of Ireland are only found in perfidious Albion, and among the toadies and tories on this side of the water. Britain still pursues the same policy of attempting to annihilate our race. We continue a thorn in her side. We stand as a living example to all the world of her perfidious treatment. Her days are soon to be numbered. Her course is nearly spent. Her greatness and glory was almost destroyed by a puny war, and when Ireland's sons gather under some strong hand in the future, it will be an easy matter to drive from the ancient Isle this perfidious enemy, restore again the beauties of the race, the purity of our men and women, and the lofty aspirations of the glorious Irish nation."

A PRESBYTERIAN CLERGYMAN'S SENTIMENT.

Rev. J. Gray Bolton, D. D., a well-known Presbyterian clergyman of Philadelphia, Pa., wrote, on January 16, 1897, in response to an invitation to be present at the institution of the American-Irish Historical Society: "I assure you that I am in hearty accord with the purpose of your organization. The Irish race owe it to themselves and their successors to leave a united history of an undivided people in America. One of the noblest characteristics of the Irishman is that he is religious; and has enough of religion to be willing to fight for it. But God forbid that this should in any way hinder in telling the united story of our people.

"The Irish Catholic and the Irish Presbyterian have more than once stood together for liberal government in Ireland. And the Irish Presbyterian and the Irish Catholic stood together here when Washington was leading the people from the yoke of oppressive taxation without representation. The Irish-American has a place and a name in this glorious country of ours, and as we fought for our freedom and then for the Union, we will live,—and, if need be, fight, side by side, to maintain it."

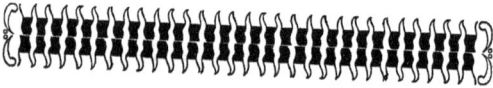

A GENERAL INDEX.

ERRATA.—On page 6, twenty-first line, for were read where; page 7, third line, for Chamber's read Chambers'; pages 11, 17, for Argylshire read Argyllshire; page 21, for Dunbarton (Dumbarton) read Dunbar.

www.ingramcontent.com/pod-product-compliance
Lightning Source LLC
Chambersburg PA
CBHW052209270326
41931CB00011B/2287